PUBLIC & PR[illegible]
WRITI[illegible]

A High Beginner Text

BRIAN ALTANO

Cover image: © Isabella Altano

www.kendallhunt.com
Send all inquiries to:
4050 Westmark Drive
Dubuque, IA 52004-1840

ISBN 978-1-4652-6730-6

Printed in the United States of America

Dedications

To Al McDowell, a professor of integrity and dedication, a mentor and a friend.

To Isabella, the most important person in my life and the source of all my creativity.

CONTENTS

CHAPTER 1 Beginnings 1

Unit 1: Getting Acquainted 2

Unit 2: Introducing Yourself 4

Unit 3: Word Processing 6

CHAPTER 2 The Basics 9

Unit 1: Parts of Speech 10

Unit 2: Writing the Paragraph: A Step-by-Step Method 18

Unit 3: The Paragraph and the Topic Sentence 18

Unit 4: Rules for Paragraphs and Correction Symbols 23

Unit 5: The Peer Review Sheet 25

CHAPTER 3 Private Writing 27

Unit 1: The Diary 28

Unit 2: The Journal 29

Unit 3: The Spelling, Vocabulary, and Grammar Notebook 32

CHAPTER 4 Public Writing: The Who, Why, and How 39

Unit 1: Audience 40

Unit 2: Purpose 41

Unit 3: Order 42

CHAPTER 5 Spatial Order 43

Unit 1: Describing Places 44

Unit 2: Describing People 65

Unit 3: Describing Objects and Situations 87

CHAPTER 6 Chronological Order 111

Unit 1: Narration Writing 112

Unit 2: Giving Advice and Directions: Process Paragraphs 134

CHAPTER 7 Ascending and Descending Order 159

Opinion Writing 160

CHAPTER 8 Block Organization (Back and Forth Order) 183

Unit 1: Making Comparisons 184

Unit 2: Cause and Effect 220

Journal Types

The Travel Journal 61

The Interesting Person Journal 83

The Food Journal 105

The Dream Journal 130

The English Conversation Journal 154

The Issue Journal 180

The Television and Movie Journal 217

The Computer and Cellphone Use Journal 248

Paragraph Types

Description 45

Narration 113

Process 135

Opinion 161

Comparison 185

Cause and Effect 221

CHAPTER 1

Beginnings

UNIT 1: GETTING ACQUAINTED

UNIT 2: INTRODUCING YOURSELF

UNIT 3: WORD PROCESSING

INTERVIEWING A CLASSMATE

For this assignment, you will interview a classmate and write a paragraph about this person. Ask some of the following questions, write down the answers, and use the information to write a description paragraph.

What is your name?

Where are you from? Where were you born?

When did you come to the United States?

How long have you been here?

Do you have any brothers and sisters?

What does your father do?

What does your mother do?

Where do they live?

Do you have a job?

What do you do (job)?

What do you do for fun? (Do you have any hobbies?)

What do you do on the weekend?

What is your favorite American food?

What is the best thing about America?

Born

Born is used in the *passive voice* and usually in the **past tense**. You must combine a past tense form of *to be* (was or were) with the past participle *born*:

I was born in 1982.
She was born in Cuba.
We were born in the spring.
They were born in Korea.

Question:
Where were you born?
What year was he born?

(In the question, the subject goes between the be-verb and born.)

Do Not Ask
How old are you?
How much do you make? (salary)
How much did your house cost? (if this person owns a house)

MY NEW FRIEND
I would like to introduce my new friend, ________________. He (She) comes from ______________.
He (She) came to the United States _______ months (years) ago. (continue ...)

© Brian J. Altano

Writing Assignment

Describe the Illustration

Write a short biography of the man in the illustration. Tell about his life, his interests, and his skills. Where does he live? What does he do? What is his family like? Invent a life story for him.

Unit 2: Introducing Yourself

How can you describe yourself? There are certain concepts that define you. The two parts of speech used the most are nouns and adjectives. Study the vocabulary in the accompanying chart. Discuss the words with the class to make sure that you understand all of them.

IDENTIFICATION CHART: VOCABULARY

CONCEPT	NOUN	ADJECTIVE
Gender	a woman, a man	female, male
Religion	a Jew, a Christian, a Muslim, a Hindu, a Buddhist, an atheist (capital letters except atheist)	Jewish, Christian, Muslim, Hindu, Buddhist
Nationality	an American, a Korean, a French person, a Russian, a Colombian, an Indian, a Chinese person, a Dominican, a Pole (a Polish person), a Cuban, a Greek, an Albanian	American, Korean, French, Russian, Colombian, Indian, Chinese, Ecuadorian, Dominican, Polish, Cuban, Greek, Albanian, Honduran, Brazilian, Italian, Spanish
Family	mother, father, sister, brother, cousins, uncles and aunts, grandmother, grandfather	large family, small family
Profession (job)	a student, a cashier, a cook, a waiter/waitress/waitperson, a mechanic, a teacher, a teacher's assistant, a nurse, a clerk, an accountant	
Personality		friendly, outgoing, shy, serious, funny, dedicated, lazy, energetic, hard-working, sad, happy, boring, traditional, helpful, religious
Physical	a blond, a brunette, a redhead (only for women)	tall, short, thin, slender, fat, chubby blond, brown, red, black, grey, and white hair
Hobbies	photography, dancing, sports, reading, computers, travel, art, music, film, hiking, bicycling, social networking, shopping, jogging, working out, video games	
Age	a teenager, a senior (citizen), an adult	21 years old, middle-aged, mature
Race	an Asian, a Hispanic, an African-American, a Caucasian, an American-Indian	Asian, Hispanic, African American, Caucasian, Indian (yellow, black, white, red)
Educational and career goals	hospitality and service industry, healthcare, IT, education, arts, law, science	

Writing Assignment

1. Fill out the identification chart to describe yourself.

CONCEPT	NOUN	ADJECTIVE
Gender		
Religion		
Nationality		
Family		
Profession (job)		
Personality		
Physical		
Hobbies		
Age		
Race		
Educational and career goals		

2. You gave background information to your partner in the *Interviewing a Classmate* activity. Now it is time to introduce yourself in writing to your professor and your classmates. Use the identification chart to write a paragraph in which you present information to give a clear picture of your personality and your interests.

WORKING WITH MICROSOFT WORD

To start Microsoft Word

1. Turn on the computer. (Press the On/Off button on your computer and the button on the monitor.)
2. Point the mouse arrow at the button at the bottom left of the screen called **"Start."**
3. Move the cursor to **"Programs"** and click the left mouse button.
4. Move the cursor to **"Microsoft Word"** and click the left mouse button.

Looking over the Word Desktop

The screen has several useful tools at your disposal:

A. **Title Bar:** Top of the screen; contains the document title after you save it; when you first write it says "Microsoft Word Document 1."

B. **Menu Bar:** Second band at the top of the screen; contains File, Edit, View, Insert, Format, Tools, Table, Window, and Help. If you click any of these words, a menu will drop down with commands you might use to manage your work.

C. **Standard Toolbar:** Third band from the top of the screen; contains several pictures or "icons" which will cause your computer to perform certain functions if you point to them with the cursor and click the left mouse button. The following icons help you write papers for your classes.
   1. **Page with turned corner:** opens a new document
   2. **Open file folder:** opens a previously saved document
   3. **Floppy diskette:** saves your document
   4. **Printer:** prints your document
   5. **Page with magnifying glass:** previews the document before printing
   6. **"ABC" box:** checks your spelling and grammar
   7. **Scissors:** cuts a highlighted portion out of your document
   8. **Double pages:** copies a highlighted portion of text
   9. **Clipboard with page:** pastes a highlighted and cut portion of text in a new place
   10. **Right pointing curved arrow:** undoes the last action you took

D. **Formatting Toolbar**: Fourth band from the top of the screen; contains menus and buttons that will help you format your document.
   1. **Style menu:** allows you to choose from a variety of type settings
   2. **Font menu:** allows you to choose from a variety of typefaces
   3. **Size menu:** allows you to choose from a variety of type sizes
   4. **Bold button:** click to change to bold typeface
   5. **Italics button:** click to change to italics typeface
   6. **Underline button:** click to change to underlined typeface
   7. **Left alignment button:** click to align text at the left margin
   8. **Centering button:** click to center text
   9. **Right alignment button:** click to align text at the right margin
   10. **Justification button:** click to align text to both margins

E. **Close Button:** "X" in the upper right corner of a window. Click to close the window, file, document, or program.

Writing and spacing your document

When you write in Microsoft Word, you only need to press Enter when you want to begin a new paragraph. Word will start a new line of typing automatically. However, the typing you do will be single spaced, unless you provide a command to double space your work. To do this, begin to type your essay. Type at least two lines of text. Then press the "Ctrl" (Control) key on your keyboard and the number 2, and Word will double space. "Ctrl" and 1 will return to single spacing.

Saving your work

A. The first time you save a document, you must give it a name.
   1. Open the File menu.
   2. Move the cursor to "Save As" and click; a dialog box appears.
   3. In the window entitled "**Save As**" click on the dropdown menu and save the document.
   4. In the window entitled **"File name"** type a brief title that describes the assignment, such as "Essayl" or "Personal1."
   5. In the window entitled "Save as type" be sure "Word Document" is entered (unless you need to save the document in a different word processing program to work on at home).
   6. Click the "Save" button.

B. If you have previously saved your document, merely press the diskette icon on the standard toolbar and you can resave the document. Word will save the document with the same name. If you want to change the name of your document, choose the "Save As" function, as above.

Opening a document <u>after</u> you have saved it

Once you save a document and leave Word, you can find it again by clicking on the file folder icon on the task bar. Highlight the file you wish to work on and press "Open."

Checking your spelling

A. On the Standard Toolbar, click on the **"ABC"** icon.
B. A dialog box appears and the spellchecker will automatically begin checking your document.
C. At the first word it does NOT recognize, it lists alternate spellings, if any. By clicking one of the suggestions, Word will automatically <u>change</u> the spelling or <u>ignore</u> the change and go on to the next unrecognized word.
D. Word will also highlight grammar and formatting errors. It will make suggestions for correction. You can choose whether to <u>change</u> or <u>ignore</u> the suggestion.

Printing your document

To print your document, open the File Menu and highlight "Print" and click. A dialog box appears which allows you to determine the number of copies you wish and what pages you want to print.

Closing Word and shutting down

Once your work is saved, close the Word program by clicking the **"X"** in the upper righthand corner of the screen. ***DO NOT TOUCH THE POWER BUTTON!*** *Always go to the "Start" button and click on it. Highlight "Shut Down" and click. The computer and monitor will shut off automatically.*

CHAPTER 2

The Basics

Unit 1: Parts of Speech
Unit 2: Writing the Paragraph: A Step-by-Step Method
Unit 3: The Paragraph and the Topic Sentence
Unit 4: Rules for Paragraphs and Correction Symbols
Unit 5: The Peer Review Sheet

UNIT 1: PARTS OF SPEECH

The basic construction in English is the *word.* Words join together to form *sentences.* Sentences combine to make *paragraphs.* In this book, you will learn many new vocabulary words. You will likely discover at least 500 new terms during the course. It is very important to find out as much as you can about each of the new words. One important fact is the word's *part of speech.* From the part of speech, you will find out how the word functions or works.

In English there are eight parts of speech. They may be divided into the little four parts and the big four parts. The little four are rather simple; the big four are more confusing. It is sometimes difficult to tell them apart.

The little four parts of speech:

pronoun	**article**
preposition	**conjunction**

The big four parts of speech:

verb	**noun**
adverb	**adjective**

Each chapter in the book focuses on one of these parts of speech. The following is a general introduction.

THE LITTLE FOUR PARTS OF SPEECH

Pronoun

A pronoun stands for a noun. It may refer to a noun previously mentioned. For example: *John* gave *the book* to *his sister* may be rephrased as: *He* gave *it* to *her.* The antecedent of *He* is *John.* The antecedent of *it* is *the book.* The antecedent of *her* is *his sister.*

Function: A pronoun may be:

1. a subject
2. an object
3. a relative pronoun
4. a possessive

1. Subject
   - 1a. **He** is a nurse.
   - 1b. **They** work at an internet café.

2. Object
   - 2a. Eun Hye saw **him** yesterday at a dance club.
   - 2b. Maya talked to **them** about the new hip-hop CD.
   - 2c. Please help **me**. I am falling down.

3. Relative 3a. I can't stand people **who** lie.
   3b. The woman **whose** hair is green and red is an art student.
   3c. The car **that** Seong Dong bought is ten years old.

4. Possessive 4a. The soccer ball is **his.**
   4b. The cell phone on the table is **mine.**

Note: The possessive pronoun **always** stands alone. It is **never** followed by a noun. Usually, it is the last word in the sentence. The possessive pronouns are *mine, yours, his, hers, ours,* and *theirs.*

Article
There are only three articles in English: a, an, and the. **Definite** (the) or **indefinite** (a, an) articles (i.e., ***a*** before a consonant sound and ***an*** before a vowel sound) are placed before a noun.

1. **The** Uggs boots cost $250.
2. I always drink **a** cup of tea in **the** afternoon.
3. Armando bought **an** ugly striped shirt.
4. Choon Hee studies at **a** university in Seattle, Washington.
   [*Note*: the ***u*** in university has a consonant sound, so *a*, not *an,* is used.]
5. Isabel Fonseca is **an** honest woman.
   [The word *honest* begins with a consonant (h), but the *h* is silent, so the article is **an.**]

Preposition
A preposition is a linking word. It is used with verbs (two-word verbs) in many idiomatic expressions. Most commonly, it is used in a phrase.

Function: Prepositions usually indicate direction or position. They are used in phrases (a prepositional phrase = *preposition [+article] + noun*). When the preposition ***to*** is followed by the base form of the verb, the verb is in the ***infinitive*** form.

1. The teacher walked **out** the back door **of** the classroom.
2. My father lives **in** Algeria **in** the winter and **in** Illinois **in** the summer.
3. Mattie works **in** the afternoon.
4. His cousin will be **in** the army **until** October.
5. Sun Hee called her ex-boyfriend **at** 6:00 a.m. **to** wake him **up**.
6. I always heat **up** my pizza **in** the microwave **for** forty seconds.

Conjunction
Function: A conjunction joins phrases or clauses. You should use ***and*** to add information; use ***but, yet, although,*** and ***though*** for contrast; and use ***so, because,*** and ***since*** for result.

1. Pedro lives in Hallendale **and** works in Miami.
2. Ivona is very intelligent, **but** she is sometimes lazy.

3. My little brother always wanted a dog, **yet** he never takes it for a walk.
4. **Although** I am very tired, I will not quit until I finish.
5. **Though** it was cold, they went for a long walk.
6. Pavel speaks four languages, **so** he is an interpreter.
7. Patricia is staying home **because** she is sick.
8. **Since** it is raining, we will not go to the park.

THE BIG FOUR PARTS OF SPEECH

Verb

A verb provides a great deal of information. It tells **tense** (*time*: present, past, future; *tense:* simple, progressive, perfect, perfect progressive), **voice** (active/passive/imperative), and **number** (singular/plural). There are also auxiliary or helping verbs.

1. Action
   - 1a. I **ate** delicious samosas in an Indian restaurant.
   - 1b. The thief **ran** away from the police officer.
   - 1c. Prof. MacDougall **writes** books and articles.

2. State of being
   - 2a. Dr. Co **is** a cardiologist.
   - 2b. The Williams sisters **won** the doubles championship.
   - 2c. Ms. Ibanez **was** the best teacher in my high school.

3. Passive voice
   - 3a. Dr. Martin Luther King **was murdered** in Memphis, Tennessee, in 1968.
   - 3b. The World Trade Center **was destroyed** in 2001.
   - 3c. Jay-Z **was born** in Brooklyn in 1969.

4. Auxiliary
   - 4a. Vidhi's boyfriend **is** baking a cake for her birthday party.
   - 4b. Tomás **has** eaten four slices of pizza.
   - 4c. Yousef and Talal **are** watching the video on YouTube.

5. Imperative
   - 5a. **Be** quiet! Everyone is trying to concentrate on the exam.
   - 5b. Don't **stare** at the dragon tattoo on her leg.
   - 5c. **Don't hang** up! **Stay** on the phone. **Listen** to me.

Noun

A noun is a person, place, or thing. It is also a concept, a mood, or an attitude.

Function: A noun is a **subject** or an **object.** As the subject, it usually goes near the beginning of the sentence, just before the verb. As the object, it comes after a verb or a preposition. The noun may be compound (firefighter), common (pasta), collective (the army), or proper (Elizabeth).

1. **Paola** is from **Rio de Janeiro**.
2. **Coffee** is more expensive than **tea.**

3. **The army** lost the **war**.
4. **Jealousy** is not a sign of **love**.
5. My **brother** is a fantastic **cook**.
6. The **textbook** is on the **desk**.
7. The **firefighter** and the **police officer** were married in Houston, Texas, yesterday.
8. **Rice** is the most important food in Korean, Japanese, and Chinese cooking.
9. **Rosalita** lives with **Gustav**.
10. **Hanoi** is the capital of **Vietnam**.

Adverb
An adverb usually goes right after the verb. Many adverbs end in *ly*.

Function: An adverb modifies a verb. It may also modify another adverb or an adjective. Adverbs usually answer questions: (1) time (when?); (2) manner (how?); (3) place (where?); (4-5) degree (how much?); and (6) frequency (how often?).

The words *not, yesterday, today, tomorrow,* and *now* are adverbs; so are *here* and *there. Adverbs of frequency* also exist (*always, usually, often, sometimes, occasionally, rarely, seldom, never*). These adverbs are generally placed before the verb, but **sometimes** may go at the beginning, in the middle, or even at the end of a sentence.

1. Time	1a. Kay left **immediately** after the movie. 1b. Bar's sister is living in Chicago **now**. 1c. Mostafa leaves **early** from work on Friday.
2. Manner	2a. Marco dances **well**. 2b. The romantic writer whispers **softly**. 2c. Georgi speaks **fast** in his native language.
3. Place	3a. My cousin lives **here** in this old house. 3b. Zach is **there** in the police car. 3c. Billy always hides **here**, in the closet, when they play hide-and-seek.
4. Describing an adjective	4a. Hank has a **very** *big* nose. 4b. Andrew is **incredibly** *unlucky*. 4c. Mi Lan's fingernails are **too** *long*.
5. Describing an adverb	5a. Marta talks **very** *fast* when she is nervous. 5b Ned ran **extremely** *quickly* to his next class. 5c. The professor came **too** *late* to see the movie.
6. Frequency	6a. John **sometimes** calls his ex-girlfriend at three o'clock in the morning. 6b. Antonia **frequently** drinks two cups of tea with breakfast. 6c. Hanan **always** stays up late to study for an exam.

Adjective

Adjectives are colorful words that we use to tell about a person, place, thing, or experience. When you use clear adjectives, people can get a picture of the noun you are describing.

Function: An adjective describes a noun or a pronoun. It is usually placed right before the noun. It may go after a **be** verb. Possessives that go before a noun are adjectives. Colors are also adjectives, and so are numbers.

1. The **long** program was **boring**.
2. Krista has **blond** hair.
3. The **Brazilian** band played **excellent** music.
4. The **hungry** man ate **four** hamburgers.
5. The **old** sailor told an **interesting** story about gigantic sea monsters.
6. **His** dog is **black** and **grey**.
7. Teresa washes **her** hands **six** times a day.
8. **Many** people like **spicy** food, but I prefer **bland** food.

PARTS OF SPEECH AND THEIR FUNCTIONS
REVIEW AND ANALYSIS CHART

PART OF SPEECH	FORM (ENDINGS)	FUNCTION	POSITION IN THE SENTENCE	NOTES
Pronoun	I, you, she, he, it, we, they, me, him, her, us, them, mine, theirs, yours	Stands for the noun: 1. Subject 2. Object 3. Relative 4. Possessive	1. **Subject:** Before the verb 2. **Object:** After the verb 3. **Relative:** After a noun 4. **Possessive:** After the verb (That pen is ***mine.***)	**Relative pronouns** introduce a new clause: - I know a woman **who** drives a taxi. - The man **whose** car is parked there works in a bar.
Article	the, a, an	Definite (*the*) and indefinite (*a, an*)	Placed before a noun (a woman) or before an adjective + noun (the large city)	Use **a** before consonant sounds (a university, a diner); use **an** before vowel sounds (an honest woman, an ugly dog)
Preposition	in, at, on, from, between, to, for, about, up, across, out	Indicates position or direction	May begin a sentence, follow a verb, or come at the end of a sentence	Often introduces a **prepositional phrase** (Prep. + Art. + Noun) (i.e., in the kitchen)

Conjunction	and, but, so, for, yet, because, since, although, though,	Transition word to another clause, phrase, or word	Usually placed at the end of one clause and before the subject of the next clause	When there are **five** words before **and, but so,** and **yet**, place a comma before the word. Otherwise, the comma is optional
Verb	-ed, -ing, -en, -ate, -ize, -fy, -gress, -mit	1. Action 2. General fact 3. State of being	1. After the subject in a normal (declarative) sentence 2. Inverted order in a question (interrogative sentence) [verb first, subject second] - (i.e., **Are you busy**?)	A verb shows: - **tense** (past, present, future) (simple, perfect, progressive, perfect prog.) - **number** (sing./plural) - **voice** (mood) - active - passive - imperative
Noun	-ity, -ide, -ude, -logy, -or, -ess, -er, -ant, -tion	1. Subject 2. Object a. of verb b. of preposition	1. **Subject**: At the beginning of the sentence, before the verb 2. **Object**: After the verb or preposition (Mary *called* **John**. Usha works *in a* **bank**.)	- Person, place, or thing - Count or non-count nouns (book, car, bread, water) - Abstract nouns (honor, humility, jealousy) - Collective nouns (team, army, gang) - Compound nouns (letter carrier, flight attendant)
Adverb	-ly (also **very**, **too**, and **so**) Adverbs answer the questions **how? when? where? how often?**	Modifies: 1. a verb 2. an adverb (Todd arrived **too** late.) 3. an adjective (Inge is **so** sad.)	1. After a verb (Gee Mee drives **safely**.) 2. Before another adverb (Nick ran **very** fast.) 3. Before an adjective (Sami is **very** ill.)	Adverbs of **frequency** (always, usually, often, sometimes, seldom, rarely, never), usually **go before** the verb. **Not, here, there, yesterday, today, now, tomorrow** are also adverbs
Adjective	-ful, -ous, -cal, -less, -ic, -ive **Numbers** and **colors** are adjectives.	Modifies a noun or a pronoun	1. Immediately before the noun it modifies 2. After a form of the verb **be**	The **sick** boy cried. The **grey** cat meowed. Pam is never **bored**. Joe was **interested** in the book.

Exercises on parts of speech

Exercise 1

In the following sentences, give the part of speech of each word. For verbs, indicate tense, number, and voice. For nouns, indicate function (subject or object).

1. In the evening, the busy worker drinks two cups of coffee.
2. My sister is very happy to work at the mall.
3. The energetic teacher works in a large school.
4. The cashier sat patiently on a high chair in the register.
5. Sometimes Juan eats two lunches, but he jogs three times a week.
6. The people in Romania and Hungary are very friendly.
7. My elderly uncle sings very well.
8. The tired woman smiled happily after the store closed.
9. Marco reads easily, but he has many problems with geometry.
10. Roscoe saw many interesting buildings in Cleveland yesterday.
11. The fantastic movie lasted three hours.
12. The chef was angry because he burned two large steaks.
13. Han Bo won the lottery, but the prize was not large.
14. Kathleen is a famous engineer, and her brother is a respected dentist.
15. The weather was warm, so the nurse left his heavy coat in the closet.

Exercise 2

Insert a word in the blank, and indicate its part of speech.

1. The _________ manager walked __________ out of the office.
2. The tall ___________ yelled at the ____________ soccer player.
3. The veterinarian wore a _________ suit.
4. In ____ evening, my friends ______________ around the lake three times.
5. It was snowing, ____ we didn't go to the _________.
6. ______ old dog ______________ with his owner.
7. Jeremy was ________ late, so he ______ all the way from the parking lot to the office.
8. I love ____ eat pizza, _________, and French fries.
9. My little brother __________ two _________ every afternoon.
10. On _________, Joe and his _________ go to _________.
11. Helmer bought an __________ coat.
12. The new CD is ________. I love _______ song.
13. Myeong Go, please turn ______ the radio. We are _________ to sleep.
14. The basketball team ______ five times a ______ during ____ season.
15. Carol loves him, _____ he doesn't _________ her.

Unit 2: Writing the Paragraph: A Step-by-Step Method

Follow these rules in your writing

1. Write or type your name and the date in the top right corner of the page.
2. Write a title in the middle of the top line.
3. **Indent** your first sentence. If you type, press the TAB key once. If you write with a pen or pencil, begin your sentence two inches from the left margin (the red line down the page).
4. Write on one line. Skip a line. Write on the next line. If you are typing, use double space (in Microsoft, click on Format, Paragraph, Line Spacing [Double]). This gives the instructor room to make corrections and write comments.
5. When you finish a sentence, place a period. Then leave space before you begin your next sentence. If you are typing, press the space key twice before you begin your next sentence.
6. Begin each new sentence with a capital letter.
7. Leave room at the end of the line. Do not write all the way to the edge of the page. If you are typing in Word or another word processing program, do not press Enter at the end of the line. The program automatically brings the text to the next line.
8. If you are handwriting the paragraph, follow the margin line (the red line) on the left. Do not write on the other side of the margin.
9. Do not hyphenate words at the end of the line. Hyphenation rules are very complicated in English. Start a longer word on the next line. Again, a word processing program automatically brings the text to the next line.
10. Make sure to write a strong topic sentence and conclusion.

Unit 3: The Paragraph and the Topic Sentence

A *paragraph* is a group of related sentences on one topic. There are three parts of a paragraph:

1. the topic sentence (the introduction)
2. the body (supporting details)
3. the conclusion (the closing)

Topic sentence

The topic sentence is usually the first sentence in the paragraph. It serves four important functions:

1. The topic sentence introduces the main idea of the paragraph.
2. It directs or sets the tone for the order of the sentences.
3. It indicates the type of paragraph (description, narration, process, cause and effect, comparison, opinion).
4. The topic sentence tells the subject and the point of view of the paragraph.

There are several types of topic sentences. Usually these vary according to the kind of paragraph. The following are *standard* topic sentences.

PARAGRAPH TYPE	STANDARD TOPIC SENTENCE
Description	My favorite brother Joshua has several interesting characteristics.
Narration	The time that I saved my friend's life was the proudest moment in my life.
Process	If you would like to learn to cook bulgogi, read these directions.
Comparison	There are several differences between my two English professors.
Opinion	I am strongly against capital punishment for the following reasons.

Catchy Topic Sentences

One of the purposes of the topic sentence is to draw readers into the paragraph, to attract their attention. Although this is possible with a standard topic sentence, it is probably easier with a *catchy* topic sentence—one that captures them. The following are examples of this type of topic sentence.

PARAGRAPH TYPE	CATCHY TOPIC SENTENCE
Description	Everyone thinks that my brother is too proud, but they really don't know him well.
Narration	When I stood there facing a loaded gun, I thought that I would never live to see another day.
Process	If you fall off a boat in the middle of a lake, you will probably wish that you could swim.
Comparison	Students generally like Prof. Balongo much more than Prof. Ray, but they should understand the good points of each of these criminal justice instructors.
Opinion	I believe that Ms. Wilkinson is the strongest candidate for the Senate in many, many years.

Questions as Topic Sentences

One excellent way to engage readers is to address them directly. This can be done by posing a question as the topic sentence. The question involves readers in the topic and makes them think about the subject and its relation to their own lives. The following are examples of questions as the topic sentence.

PARAGRAPH TYPE	QUESTION AS TOPIC SENTENCE
Description	Who is the most interesting person in your family?
Narration	Have you ever thought of the most embarrassing moment in your life?
Process	Have you ever wished that you could make a salad so fantastic that people always ask for seconds?
Comparison	What are the main differences between a vacation at the beach and a vacation in the mountains?
Opinion	Do you believe that America should get involved in every conflict overseas?

Topic Sentences

Exercise 1

On a separate sheet of paper or in your notebook, write a standard topic sentence for the following writing topics.

1. A description of your best friend
2. A description of the house or apartment you live in now
3. A narration about the scariest moment in your life
4. A narration about a time when you felt very proud of yourself
5. A process paragraph about how to cook a special dish
6. A process paragraph about how to get an A in writing class
7. A comparison paragraph about two of your relatives
8. A comparison paragraph about two places where you have lived
9. An opinion paragraph about your view of penalties for drug possession
10. An opinion paragraph about the best type of music

Exercise 2

On a separate sheet of paper or in your notebook, write a *catchy* topic sentence for the following writing topics.

1. A description of your cheapest relative
2. A description of the worst place that you have ever visited
3. A narration about a time that you were robbed or when you lost something
4. A narration about your first day in America
5. A process paragraph about how to organize your life
6. A process paragraph about how to save money for a special purpose
7. A comparison paragraph about two of your co-workers or friends
8. A comparison paragraph about two types of food
9. An opinion paragraph about assisted suicide
10. An opinion paragraph about the responsibility of the government for taking care of the homeless

Exercise 3

On a separate sheet of paper or in your notebook, write a question as topic sentence for the following writing topics.

1. A description of the ugliest house that you have ever seen
2. A description of the most precious (to you) object in your house
3. A narration about an interesting family trip
4. A narration about the birth of a child (your brother or sister, nephew or niece, or someone else)
5. A process paragraph about how to plant a garden or do your favorite hobby
6. A process paragraph about how to make a good impression on a new boss or on the parent of a close friend

7. A comparison paragraph about two teachers from your high school days
8. A comparison paragraph about two friends from your youth
9. An opinion paragraph about illegal immigrants in the United States
10. An opinion paragraph about the best team in your favorite sport (or the best actor or actress)

Exercise 4
Write a topic sentence for the following paragraphs. Then indicate the type of paragraph (narration, opinion, comparison, process, or description).

1. Topic sentence: ____

   First, my sister is intelligent. She always gets As in her classes. She knows how to solve problems. When I have a difficult problem in math, she explains the answer very clearly. In addition, my sister Maria is very friendly. She has many friends and acquaintances. When she goes to a party, after only fifteen minutes, she knows everyone in the room. Finally, she is quite helpful. People know that if they need assistance, they can call my sister. She will come right away. My sister is very special.

   Type of paragraph: ____________________

2. Topic sentence: ____

   First of all, buy lettuce, tomatoes, onions, olives, and cucumbers. Cut the ingredients into small pieces. Place them in a deep bowl. Then add oil and vinegar and a little pepper. Toss everything together and serve with fresh bread. If you follow my directions, you will make an excellent salad.

   Type of paragraph: ____________________

3. Topic sentence: ____

   Everything happened when I was thirteen years old. I was returning home from school when I saw a wallet on the ground. I picked it up and looked inside. There were six one-hundred dollar bills and several twenties. On the other side of the wallet, I noticed a driver's license with a photograph. I couldn't believe it. It was the principal of my middle school! The next morning I couldn't wait to get to school. As soon as I got off the bus, I walked into the principal's office. He was sitting at his desk, looking sad. I immediately took out the wallet and handed it over to him. He was shocked, and started grinning from ear to ear. He called me a very honest girl. The next day he gave me a gift certificate to a local restaurant. I took my parents and my little brother for an excellent dinner. I will never forget that day as long as I live.

   Type of paragraph: ____________________

4. Topic sentence: ______________________________

The first difference between my friend Josefa and me is our height. Josefa is as tall as a giraffe, but I am very short. When we walk together on the street, people stare at us because Josefa is twice as tall as I am. Another difference is our personalities. Josefa is sort of shy; on the other hand, I am very outgoing. I love to meet new people and to talk to everyone. Josefa takes a long time to warm up to people. The last difference between Josefa and me is our family. I have an incredibly large family: six brothers and three sisters. In addition, my grandmother lives with us and my cousins live on the next street. Josefa lives in a small house only with her mother. Despite our differences, Josefa and I are best friends.

Type of paragraph: ______________

5. Topic sentence: ______________________________

The first reason why I love to play soccer is that it is excellent exercise. I love to run, and in a soccer game I get a chance to move around for ninety minutes with only short breaks. Another excellent thing about soccer is that anyone can play. Two of my friends, Winston and Abdul, are kind of round. However, they are very good defenders. My friend Mario is very short, but he is the best player on the team. Players don't have to be really tall as in basketball or really big as in football. Finally, the last reason why I love soccer is that it is fun. Everyone loves to kick the ball, to shoot, and to score. These are the reasons why I love soccer.

Type of paragraph: ______________

Unit 4: Rules for Paragraphs and Correction Symbols

Upper Right Corner

Name → Erika Johanssen

Date → December 15, 2005

Center the Title

The Most Interesting Person in My Family

Write a strong topic sentence

Indent the first sentence

The most interesting person in my family is my brother Lars. He is twenty-eight years old, and he has a great personality. He makes everyone laugh. In fact,he is never serious. Even in church and during important examinations, he always makes jokes. He has big eyes and very large ears. He can wiggle his ears. One time my uncle told me a serious story about the war. He explained about how he got lost in a forest, and it took him two days to get out. During this conversation, my brother sat on the other side of the room, wiggling his ears and trying to make me laugh. He chose the correct job for himself. He is a writer on a television program, a comedy, of course. I really love my brother.

Leave one space after a comma

Justify the left margin

Leave a right margin

double space on the computer or write on every other line when handwriting

Leave two spaces after a period.

Write a conclusion

Begin a new sentence with a capital letter.

Hanna, My Greato-Grandmother

My great-grandmother Hanna is almost a hundred years old. From 1946 to 1972, she was professor at the University of Manila in Philippines. SHe still have long, natural, black hair. When she was 18, she marries her best friend, Hernando, who became my grandfather. They loved each other very much, they had four children. She went to the university to study physics. After she finished her studies. She became a famous proffessor. She was very professional. She loved to read long novels and she also wrote three books. She wrote them all by her self. Afterwards her husband was died, she continued to live her own. Because she is so old, so has a poor sight. Her hear is not so good, either. Her mind is very sharp. My great-grandmother is a wonderful woman.

Correction Symbols

Run-on:	run-on sentence
Tense:	you need to change the verb tense
Frag:	fragment (incomplete sentence)
Sp:	spelling mistake
Agr:	subject / verb agreement mistake [i.e. John speak; Nancy and Bill is]
^	a word is missing
¶	Start a new paragraph
ơ	remove whatever is circled [i.e. I have two pairs' of shoes (the apostrophe is not necessary)]
◡	Join the two words into one [i.e. my self (myself is one word)]
Awk	Awkward [the wording of the sentence or phrase sounds awkward, so you need to reword it]
Trans:	Write a transition to connect ideas
WC:	word choice (the word does not make sense)
Form:	word form mistake [i.e. noun form instead of adjective; verb instead of noun]
=	Capital Letter (b = B)

UNIT 5: THE PEER REVIEW SHEET

During the semester, your professor will probably ask you to bring a paragraph to class and exchange it with a partner. Your classmates are your peers, or equals. You will read over your classmate's work and make comments and perhaps corrections. Use this peer review sheet as a model. Always try to find several **positive** elements in the writing. Do not simply look for errors.

1. What do you like most about the paragraph?

2. Is there a topic sentence? Is it a good one? Why or why not?

3. Is there a strong conclusion?

4. List the specific details that the writer uses.

5. Are there verb mistakes in the composition? What type (tense, subject/verb agreement, voice)?

6. Are there other types of mistakes?

7. What parts of the paragraph need improvement?

CHAPTER 3

Private Writing

UNIT 1: THE DIARY
UNIT 2: THE JOURNAL
UNIT 3: THE SPELLING, VOCABULARY, AND GRAMMAR NOTEBOOK

There are three kinds of private writing in this book: (1) the diary, (2) the journal, and (3) the spelling, vocabulary, and grammar notebook. The diary is strictly personal. You record your daily thoughts and feelings, impressions, and ideas. The journal presents your opinions about what you read about in books, newspapers, and magazines, what you see on television or at the movies, and what you listen to on the radio or your iPod. In the spelling, vocabulary, and grammar notebook, you write down problem words, spelling rules, and grammar points.

UNIT 1: THE DIARY

You probably know the English word ***diary***. Maybe you have read a famous book that uses the word in its title, such as *The Diary of Anne Frank*. Perhaps you have kept a diary yourself sometime in your life. The English word *diary* is closely related to the Spanish word *dia*, which means "day"; a diary is a record about what you do, think, and feel every day. Often, diaries are private, almost secret. Because you record your inner thoughts, you probably don't want strangers to read it. Many diary books are even sold with a lock and key to make sure that curious people cannot open them to find out what you are thinking.

PROCESS

Write in your diary three times a week. Number and date your diary entries. Your teacher will not read the specific entries, but only check that you have done them.

POSSIBLE DIARY TOPICS

- Describe your new classmates in detail.
- How do you feel about your new teacher? (Your teacher will not read it, so don't worry.)
- What problems are you having now?
- What do you fear?
- What goals do you have for the short term (just this semester)?
- Describe your long-term goals (the next two years).
- Tell about your daily routine—that is, what do you do every day?
- Describe the best conversations that you have had in the last few weeks.
- You might talk about romance.
- Talk about your interests. What do you like to do in your free time?

Sample Diary Entry

Diary entry 1 July 18, 2015
Today was a terrible day! Everything went wrong. My alarm clock didn't ring, and I overslept. Then I made myself breakfast, but I burned the toast. I made coffee and carried it to the car. I put the coffee cup

on top of the car when I opened the door. I forgot the coffee on the car. I drove away and the cup went flying through the air. It broke on the ground. I got to class late. The teacher explained that she wanted students to come to class on time. Finally, in class I relaxed and was ready to study. But I opened my bag, and my book was not there. I forgot my book. What a disaster!

UNIT 2: THE JOURNAL

You probably also know the English word ***journal***, which is sometimes used in the name of a magazine, such as *Ladies Home Journal*, or a newspaper, such as *The Wall Street Journal*. The word *journal* is related to the French word *jour*, which also means "day," and one of its meanings is the same as the meaning of diary.

Many people keep journals, and not only because they want to improve their writing. Some want to remember their feelings and thoughts and read about them at some time in the future. Some like to read their journals to see how they have grown and changed. Some feel that if they write about their lives, they can solve their problems better. Also, some writers keep journals to practice and improve their writing, just as some artists keep pads of paper to make sketches and plans for drawings and paintings that they will do later. If your teacher asks you to keep a journal for this class, it will be for this last reason, to practice and improve your writing.

For you, as a language student, the biggest advantage of keeping a journal is that you will be able to write without worrying about making mistakes in grammar, spelling, etc. Studies have shown that even if you make mistakes when you write in your journal, the practice that you get will help you improve as a writer and make fewer mistakes when you write for others. No one knows why this improvement occurs, but it might be because journal keepers can practice their writing without worrying what anyone thinks about what they write or how they write.

You should not be afraid of saying something foolish or making a mistake in your journal if your teacher asks you to keep one. In your journal, then, you can write for yourself, and you can be quite sure that this practice will help you write better for other people.

Finally, what can you write about in your journal? You teacher might make suggestions or even give assignments for journal writing. Otherwise, you are free to write about anything. Your teacher might help you get started. In addition, each of the following chapters in this book has a section with specific types of journals.

To improve their skills, athletes practice all the time. Soccer players kick the ball and dribble time after time. Pianists do scales to keep their figures flexible. Painters make sketches before they paint a large canvas. Speakers practice making speeches again and again. Chess players play many games and study their moves. In the same way, writers improve their skills by writing a wide variety of material.

You should write in your journal for **fifteen minutes a day, four days a week**. This is a quick and easy way to improve your writing skills. Instead of just writing about your daily life (which you do in the **DIARY**), you should write about other matters, too. You should include journal entries about the *past* and about the *future*. This is another way to practice your *verb tenses.*

Don't worry about how much you write. Just write for fifteen minutes. Try to write at the same time each day so that you can develop a good habit. For example, write every morning between 7:00 and 7:15, or every evening between 9:00 and 9:15. Don't worry too much about spelling or grammar. Journal writing is free writing and should be a smooth and continuous activity.

Be creative. You can use the topics suggested in the book, or you can make up topics of your own. Keep a separate notebook for your journal. A journal is a written record. It presents your impressions, feelings, and thoughts about everyday life. In the journal you can also write your opinion about current issues.

Journal writing should be a ***daily habit***. You will improve more when you are serious about writing every day. You probably speak and read more than you write. The only way for writing to become "natural" is to do it as much as possible. This is the best way to improve.

If your days are repetitive, you might find that you are repeating yourself in your journal. To avoid this, write **reaction journals.** Read the newspaper or watch the news and write on what is happening in the world. Talk about an interesting movie that you saw last weekend or a good television program that you watched. Write about the websites that you regularly visit, the people you meet on Facebook, and the videos you watch on YouTube.

The following is the process for journal writing. Continue this activity through the whole semester.

In this book you will keep many types of journals: a food journal, a lying journal, a dream journal, a cell phone use journal, an English conversation journal, and a day-trip journal. The variety will (hopefully) keep you interested and writing.

Process for Journals

1. Use a separate notebook for your journal.
2. Begin every new journal entry on a new page.
3. Number your journals and put the date at the top.
4. Try to write in your journal at the same time every day.
5. Write for fifteen minutes.
6. Do not worry too much about grammar or spelling. Try to write your ideas down.
7. After fifteen minutes, stop. You will have time to write again tomorrow.

SUGGESTED JOURNAL TOPICS

1. Describe your best friend from the first grade.
2. Describe the house where you live now.
3. Describe the house where you used to live.
4. Describe a pet that you have (or had).
5. Describe the best teacher you have ever had.
6. Describe the worst teacher you have ever had.
7. Describe your best friend now.
8. Describe who you will marry (or who your son or daughter will marry).
9. Tell about the most exciting day in your life.
10. Tell about your scariest experience.
11. Tell a funny story.
12. Tell about something that happened to you because of a mistake in the language.
13. Have you ever been really late for something? (tell the story)
14. Narrate your activities from last weekend.
15. What happened during your most enjoyable vacation?

The following sample journal entry is a reaction to a newspaper article. It presents a personal opinion, but it is based on something that you read.

Sample Journal Entry

Journal entry 1 July 19, 2015
I read an article in the newspaper today. It was about a man who jumps from cliffs. He lives in Hawaii. In a place where many tourists go, there is a high cliff. The water is 90 feet below. The man dives from the cliff, and the tourists give him money. He jumps 15 times every day. He earns a lot of money. I think this is a crazy job. It is very dangerous. I am afraid of heights, so I don't think this is a job for me. But he doesn't have to go to an office or a store, and he has no boss. I think I would die on this job. After all, I can't even swim.

The diaries and journals will be collected once per month. The collection dates for the semester are: __________, __________, __________, and __________.

UNIT 3: THE SPELLING, VOCABULARY, AND GRAMMAR NOTEBOOK

SPELLING

Spelling in English is very difficult. Of course, there are some rules, but is seems as if there are just as many exceptions to these rules. You must accept the fact that you **will** make spelling mistakes. This is natural.

However, it is what you do after a spelling mistake that is important. You should write the word in a separate notebook. Keep a running list of words that you have had trouble with. The more you write words down, the better chance that you have of really learning correct spelling. Also, after you learn the correct spelling of a word, try to use it often so that you can reinforce the right way of writing it. Add to your spelling notebook every day, and read over it at least once a week. You might also include spelling rules in this journal.

VOCABULARY

If you want to develop a powerful vocabulary, you have to work hard. The more work you do, the more you will learn. When you find a new word, you should write it down in the Spelling, Vocabulary, and Grammar Notebook. Include as much information as you can about the new word. Your entry should look like this:

hack: v, (-) to break into someone's computer system.
The tech person *hacked* into the company's email system and read employee email.

Write the word and give the part of speech. Then tell whether the word has a *positive*, *negative*, or *neutral* connotation. Tell if there are any prefixes, suffixes, or roots that help you find its meaning. Finally, use the new word in your own sentence. Here is another example:

promotion: n, (+) [the prefix *pro* means "forward"] movement upwards in your career.
My sister received a *promotion* to vice-president in the bank.

Notice that in this entry, the prefix *pro* is described.

GRAMMAR

As you know, grammar is a set of rules and models. When you find a new grammar rule, write in down in the Spelling, Vocabulary, and Grammar Notebook. Always include a sample sentence to reinforce what you have learned. For example:

Rule: Don't use a double negative. Change one of the parts to positive.
I *don't* have *no* money.
You must change this sentence in one of two possible ways:

1. I have no money. [The verb is now in the positive form.]
2. I don't have any money. [The negative *no* is replaced by the positive *any*.]

The Spelling, Vocabulary, and Grammar Notebook is a study book. Read over the three sections to help you remember words, rules, and models. Pay close attention. It is normal to make mistakes. What you do with your mistakes is important in the learning process. Learn from your mistakes, and try not to repeat them.

The Spelling, Vocabulary, and Grammar Notebook

___________	___________	___________
___________	___________	___________
___________	___________	___________
___________	___________	___________
___________	___________	___________
___________	___________	___________
___________	___________	___________
___________	___________	___________
___________	___________	___________
___________	___________	___________
___________	___________	___________
___________	___________	___________
___________	___________	___________
___________	___________	___________
___________	___________	___________
___________	___________	___________
___________	___________	___________
___________	___________	___________

CHAPTER 4

Public Writing

THE WHO, WHY, AND HOW

UNIT 1: AUDIENCE
UNIT 2: PURPOSE
UNIT 3: ORDER

UNIT 1: AUDIENCE

Part Three discussed private writing: the diary, the journal, and the spelling, vocabulary, and grammar notebook. Most writing, of course, is not done only for the writer to read. One reason why you are going to school is to learn to write in English for others. It is this complicated and very difficult kind of writing that is the topic of the rest of this book. You will learn to answer three basic questions when you write:

1. Who is your audience?
2. Why are you writing?
3. What order should you use to organize your paragraph?

WHO IS YOUR AUDIENCE?

One of the first concerns of the writer is the reader. The intended reader of a piece of writing is called the *audience.* The audience is the WHO in the writing process. There are many characteristics of an audience that can affect the writer. Writers must consider the *age* of the reader: people speak and write differently when they are addressing children than they do when they are addressing adults. What are some other characteristics of the audience that the writer must think about? *Knowledge level* is an important consideration. You will not write in the same way for an audience of college students who major in psychology as you would if your audience was made up of farmers or mechanics. What the audience knows about your subject will alter your presentation. You will have to explain much more and provide many more details for an audience who is not familiar with a topic. *Closeness* to the writer is another aspect that affects the way you write. You write differently to close friends than you do to someone you have just met. Is there a *shared experience* with the audience? That is, do you share some of the same characteristics? *Gender* might be important because men and women may respond differently to subjects and methods of presentation. *Nationality* might also be important. When you describe your capital city, you will write differently if your audience is composed of other people from your country or if it is made up of Americans who have never been there. Finally, the *religion* and *political affiliation* of your audience may also play a role in the way that you write.

To summarize, here is a list of characteristics of your audience that you should keep in mind when you are writing:

- age
- knowledge level about the topic
- closeness to the writer
- gender
- nationality
- religion and political affiliation

EXERCISES ON AUDIENCE

1. Write two emails. One is to your best friend. Explain why you cannot go to dinner with him or her tonight. Another is to your teacher. Tell why you are unable to come to class tomorrow afternoon.

Did you use a different tone because of your audience? Were you friendlier in the first and more formal in the second?

2. Write two letters. In the first, explain why you are studying English in the United States. Your audience is your eight-year-old cousin. The second letter is to a millionaire who might want to fund your education if your reasons for studying are acceptable. Again, analyze the two letters and find differences in the way you write.
3. Write two short letters. One is to your mother or father asking for money. Another is to the Director of Financial Aid at your college. You are writing for the same reason as the first letter, but to a different audience. Analyze how the two letters differ.

UNIT 2: PURPOSE

There are at least three possible purposes for writing material that is meant to be read by another. The writer wants to *entertain*, to *inform*, or to *influence* the reader's thoughts, feelings, or actions. Usually, writers are trying to do all three. After all, every writer wants to entertain the reader, because no one wants to be boring. It is also nearly impossible to write anything without giving some information. Also, all writers want to convince the reader that what they have written is sensible and worth reading.

Certain types of writing are clear examples of each purpose. The writer of a mystery story gives the reader information and wants to make the reader believe that the events of the story could really happen. But most of all, the writer is trying to entertain the audience by creating interest and excitement. A police officer writing a report of an automobile accident should think very little about entertaining or persuading the reader. Instead the officer should concentrate on communicating information clearly and accurately. Candidates for election, when writing a speech, want to give information about themselves and be entertaining. Most of all, they want to persuade others to vote for them.

To summarize, there are three major reasons for writing:

- to entertain
- to inform
- to influence

EXERCISES ON PURPOSE

1. Tell the story of something funny that happened to you because of a mistake in language that you made. Analyze the way that you write this paragraph. Is it funny? Do you try to entertain the audience?
2. In a paragraph, explain what you will do on the next major holiday that is usually celebrated in your country. Assume that your audience is an American who knows very little about your country or your culture.
3. Write the same paragraph for an audience composed of people from your country. Is the information that you provided the same in both paragraphs? Do you provide more details in one or the other?

4. How do you feel about hunting? Write a paragraph in which you either defend hunting as an acceptable recreational activity or attack it as a terrible, primitive action. Try to persuade your audience to come over to your opinion. Support your ideas with strong proof.

UNIT 3: ORDER

The public writing portion of this book is divided into four chapters:

1. Spatial Order
2. Chronological Order
3. Ascending and Descending Order
4. Block Organization [Back and Forth Order]

Spatial order writing will be used to organize paragraphs of description. You will describe people, places, objects, and situations. You use chronological order to write narration paragraphs, in which you tell stories, and in process paragraphs, where you give instructions. Ascending and descending order is used in opinion writing. You present reasons to support your ideas to try to change your audience's mind. Finally, you write in block organization, or back and forth order, in both comparison/contrast and cause/effect and paragraphs.

You will practice these methods of organization in all of your writing throughout the rest of the course.

CHAPTER 5

Spatial Order

Unit 1: Describing Places
Unit 2: Describing People
Unit 3: Describing Objects and Situations

Special and Interesting Places

In 1271, the Venetian Marco Polo set sail for China with his father and uncle. He met the emperor, the Great Kublai Khan, and received an interesting job offer. Marco had to travel around Khan's vast empire and visit many cities. Then he returned to the emperor's court. The traveler had to explain all about places that Kublai Khan had never seen. What a difficult task! Describing a place well means to capture its spirit and its essence. Because one place is different from the next, different vocabulary words and structures are necessary. With his ability to describe places, Marco Polo satisfied the Great Khan and earned respect and praise.

PARAGRAPH CHART FOR DESCRIBING PLACES: SPATIAL ORDER

<table>
<tr><td>Verb tenses used</td><td>1. The simple present tense
a. regular verbs: add -s in the third-person singular
2. The present progressive (present continuous)
a. am, is, or are + the -ing form of the verb
b. used for continuous action at this moment</td></tr>
<tr><td>Organization</td><td>Spatial Order
The organization of items by space
In the description, use progressive movement. For example, go from left to right to describe a room. Go from far away to close or from bottom to top to describe a monument or a building. Walk through the rooms of the house and describe them in order.</td></tr>
<tr><td>Discourse markers: prepositions of place;

prepositional phrases (prep + art + noun)</td><td>inside · in the center · to/on the left
outside · between · to/on the right
behind · in front of · on top above
above · on · below
beneath · next to · near
in the corner · on the table · under the bed
over the door · next to the lamp · behind the couch</td></tr>
<tr><td>Topic sentence</td><td>In the topic sentence, you should:
1. name the place
2. give your general impression
The campus of Johnson Community College is a compact urban environment.
My brother Daniel's room is so messy that you can get lost in there.
The Dunkin' Donuts at the entrance to the student center is an early-morning social gathering place.</td></tr>
<tr><td>Concluding sentence</td><td>In the conclusion, you give your final impression of the place you are describing.
I will never forget my bedroom in our first house.
It is easy to understand why the Arch in St. Louis is such a magical place.</td></tr>
</table>

Grammar in Context

SUBJECT–VERB AGREEMENT

One of the most important aspects of proper grammar in description paragraphs is the agreement between the **subject** of the sentence and the **verb**. Mistakes in agreement are common, but you can correct them easily and quickly. There are several rules for subject and verb agreement, and we will study them in the Grammar in Context section of Units I and II.

There is* and *there are

Especially when we describe a place, as in this unit, we are very likely to begin sentences with the word ***there***. It is a peculiar word. Did you know when *there* is used as the subject of the sentence, it is a *pronoun*? Is it singular or plural? Actually, *there* can be used in either the singular or the plural form. Most of the time, *there* is followed by a form of the verb *to be* (*is*, *are*, *was*, *were*, *will be*). We must be very careful which form of *to be* to use. Let's analyze a few sentences.

There usually begins the sentence. It is followed by a form of the verb *to be*. Whether we use the singular or the plural verb depends on the words that follow the verb. For example:

> There (is / are) many students in this room.

Which verb form should we use? Look at the words after the verb: *many students*. This is a plural noun. Therefore, we must use the verb *are*. **There are many students in this room** is correct. Now let's look at another example:

> There (is / are) a bird in the kitchen.

Again, look at the words after the verb. Here we have a singular noun: *bird*. For this reason, we use the verb *is*. The correct sentence reads: **There is a bird in the kitchen.**

Pay particular attention to count and non-count nouns. Plural nouns take **are**. Singular nouns and non-count nouns take **is**. Look at these examples:

> There (is / are) some coffee in the refrigerator.
> There (is / are) two dirty cups on the table.

The first sentence uses the noun **coffee** after the verb. **Coffee** is *non-count*, so the verb should be **is**. In the second sentence, **cups** is a *count* noun and it is in the plural form; as a result, we use the verb **are.**

The same rules for subject and verb agreement with *there* apply to the past tense, where the forms of the verb *to be* are ***was*** and ***were***.

> There **were** two cats in the basement.
>
> [*cats* is a plural noun, so we use **were**]
>
> There **were** fifteen players on each team in the soccer game.
>
> [*players* is plural]
>
> There **was** a soldier on the train.
>
> [solider is singular, so we use **was**]
>
> There **was** a terrible hurricane in Florida last year.
>
> [hurricane is a singular noun]

In the future tense, there are no choices to make. The form ***will be*** is used for both singular and plural nouns.

> There **will be** a big surprise party for Jorge's birthday.
>
> There **will be** two examinations in grammar class this semester.

Party is singular and *examinations* is plural, but this fact does not affect the verb: *will be* is used with all subjects in the future.

Special Rule: When it introduces a count noun in the plural, *there* is followed by a plural form of *to be.* But when *there* is followed by a series of singular nouns connected by the conjunction ***and***, the singular form of *to be* is used.

> There **is** a new refrigerator and an old table in the kitchen.
>
> There **was** a string quartet and a piano soloist at the concert.
>
> There **is** a time and a place for absolute honesty.

Questions with *there is* and *there are*

The same rules apply to questions using *there is* and *there are.* As in all questions, the normal subject/verb word order is inverted. The verb goes first, followed by the subject (*there*). In the future tense, the word *there* goes between *will* and *be.*

> **Are** there many people in the restaurant?
>
> **Is** there enough cheese for everyone?
>
> **Was** there a big celebration after the World Cup finals?
>
> **Were** there any tigers and lions at the zoo?
>
> **Will** there **be** another test before the end of the month?
>
> **Will** there **be** two or three speakers at the ceremony?

© Isabella Altano

Description of the Photograph: Subject/Verb Agreement Exercise

1. Look at the photograph. Make a list of the nouns that you see.

____________	____________	____________
____________	____________	____________
____________	____________	____________
____________	____________	____________
____________	____________	____________

2. Write ten sentences using the following structures:

    a. There is + a + <u>noun</u> + prepositional phrase (preposition + article + noun).
    There is a dog on the couch. There is a sugar bowl on the table.

    b. There are + plural noun + prepositional phrase.
    There are flowers on the mantel. There are two cups on the table.

    c. Article + noun + is / are + prepositional phrase
    The dog is on the couch. The sugar bowl in on the table.

    d. Prepositional phrase + , + there is + a + <u>noun</u>
    On the couch, there is a dog.

GRAMMAR NOTES

1. In a sentence that begins with *There is*, the only article that you can use is *a/an*. You cannot use *the*.
   *There is **a** dog on the floor.*
   Incorrect: *There is **the** dog on the floor.*
2. Once you have introduced the noun, in the next sentence you can use *the*.
   *There is **a** dog on the floor. **The** dog is resting.*
3. In a sentence that begins with *There are*, no articles are used.
   There are flowers on the mantel. *There are dogs in the photograph.*
4. Remember to use a singular verb when a singular noun is followed by *and* then another noun or a list.
   There is a small dog and a large dog in the photograph.
   There is a small dog, a large dog, and a table in the photograph.

    1.
    2.
    3.
    4.
    5.
    6.
    7.
    8.
    9.
    10.

Exercise 1

Choose the correct form of the verb *to be* in parentheses.

1. There (is / are) only one reason to stay at this terrible job: it is close to home.
2. There (is / are) two places that Joe would like to visit: Antarctica and China.
3. There (is / are) a new couch, a new table, and a new lamp in the living room.
4. There (is / are) three pages of exercises to do for homework.
5. There (is / are) several interesting old buildings on the main street.
6. (Is / Are) there many biology textbooks left in the bookstore?
7. (Is / Are) there any students from Brazil in the class?
8. (Is / Are) there another way to get to school instead of Route 17?
9. (Was / Were) there a big parade yesterday in Philadelphia?
10. There (is / are) no good reason to lie to your mother.

Exercise 2

Choose the correct form of the verb *to be* in parentheses.

1. (Was / Were) there six or seven mistakes in that paragraph?
2. There (is / are) a time and a place to fool around and a time and a place to be serious.
3. There (is / are) a woman from Turkey in the cafeteria.
4. There (is / are) two table lamps in the living room.
5. There (was / were) two world wars in the twentieth century.
6. There (was / were) a big sale at Macy's last Wednesday.
7. (Is / Are) there another teacher for Reading Level 1?
8. (Was / were) there any food left after the party?
9. There (is / are) a lot of students from South America at the college now.
10. There (was / were) a rabbit in my backyard last evening.

Exercise 3

Choose the correct form of the verb *to be* in parentheses.

Sue's New Apartment

Sue is renting a new apartment. (There is / There are) three rooms. (There is / There are) a large living room. She has a couch, a love seat, and a chair in the room. (There is / There are) also two end tables and a coffee table. (There is / There are) a small kitchen next to the living room. In the kitchen, (there is / there are) a refrigerator, a stove, and a microwave. (There is / There are) also four chairs and a kitchen table. Finally (there is / there are) a medium-sized bedroom. The best thing about the bedroom is that (there is / there are) three windows, so (there is / there are) always a lot of sunlight in the room. Sue is very happy with her new apartment.

The Writing Workout Page

SPECIAL PLACES

Places leave a strong trace in our memory. We are also quite moved by colors, the arrangement of furniture, the way the sun hits a building, the gentle curve of a mountain above a lake, the clash of skyscraper and sky, and the sight of brilliant white snow on the ground. Write brief descriptions of the following places.

When you are really stressed, where do you go? Describe the place that you visit in order to relax, change your mood, and replace negative thoughts with positive ones. Even if it is not a real place (one that exists only in your mind), try to paint a word picture of your relaxing place.

____
____
____
____
____

It is your lucky day! You have just won two tickets to fly anywhere in the world, with seven nights in a five-star hotel and all your meals included. You don't have to pay a penny! So ... where will you go? Where on earth will you spend your free vacation? Describe your dream destination.

____
____
____
____
____

When you were a child, you probably had a favorite place to play. Maybe it was a room inside your house. Perhaps it was on your street, or even in a park nearby. Was it your friend's house or the schoolyard? Describe your favorite place to play when you were a kid.

____
____
____
____
____

Suppose that a friend from your country sends you an email asking you to describe the town where you are living right now. Do your best to tell your good friend about the town where you live. Concentrate on descriptive adjectives.

____
____
____
____
____

Have you ever seen a haunted house? Or perhaps a place that you avoided (or even avoid now) because you are afraid of it? Describe a place that makes you feel very uncomfortable or terrified.

____
____
____
____
____

Homework: Describe one or more of the following places:

1. Your grandma's house when you were a kid
2. Your elementary school
3. Your dream hotel
4. The classroom where you study English
5. Your favorite place to eat
6. Where you like to study
7. A good place to listen to music
8. What you see outside the window of your car or bus as you come to school
9. The view from a window in your house
10. The school library
11. The place where you like to go for a walk
12. Your favorite room in the house

Writing Assignment 1

The Dream House

© Isabella Altano

In *Home: A Short History of an Idea,* Witold Rybczynski, a professor of architecture at McGill University in Montreal, tells the reader that when he was in architecture school, his professors rarely mentioned the idea of **comfort**. The word *comfortable* means "bringing physical well-being and enjoyment," and it is seldom found in architectural magazines and plans. But we don't live in the cold rooms with few decorations shown in the photographs. To turn a *house* into a *home* we include our personal sense of style. We add objects: photographs, souvenirs from vacations, mementos of loved ones, symbols of achievement. We choose our favorite colors for the walls and the rugs. We select furniture in the store by lounging on the couch, imagining long Sunday afternoons and Thursday evenings stretched in comfort as we watch our favorite television programs or movies.

There is something about a house that reflects our deepest dreams. Lottery advertisements always tell us that when we win the $10 million prize, we can finally buy the house of our dreams. Little children "play house." They build houses out of cardboard boxes or by throwing blankets over chairs. Children play with blocks and logs and learn how to design their own living spaces. They place trees in front of the house and fields behind it. They personalize the house, and make it a home.

1. **Describing your dream house (vocabulary)**

PART OF SPEECH	CATEGORY	VOCABULARY WORDS
Noun	Rooms	Living room, family room, kitchen, dinette, dining room, bedroom, basement (finished/unfinished), study, den
Noun	Furniture	Living room: couch, loveseat, chair, rug, coffee table, end table, lamp Bedroom: bed, night table, dresser, lamp, armoire Kitchen: kitchen table, kitchen chairs, counter, appliances, stools Dining room: china closet, dining room table, sideboard, server
Noun	House parts	roof, front yard, back yard, lawn, the interior, the exterior, driveway, garage, front door, back door
Adjective	Descriptions of house and rooms	spacious, bright, airy, comfortable, crowded, cramped, relaxing
Verb	Verbs + objects	decorate (the house), furnish (the rooms), mow the lawn, plant flowers, arrange the furniture, place or put (objects in the room)

2. **Designing and drawing the house**
   On a separate sheet of paper, draw your dream house. Also, take notes about the interior and exterior. Include information about style, color, and size.

3. **Describing the house**
   Use the vocabulary box and your drawing/notes to write a ten-sentence paragraph describing your dream house.

Writing Assignment 2

Decorating a Studio Apartment

The rent in large cities such as New York, Chicago, Miami, San Francisco, and Boston is very high. As a result, many people who live alone rent *studio apartments*, single rooms that serve as kitchen, living room, and bedroom all in one. It is your assignment to decorate a studio apartment, including all the furniture that you consider necessary to live comfortably in a fifteen- by eighteen-foot space. Use the room plan provided to create your design. Then use prepositions of place to write a ten-sentence description of your studio apartment.

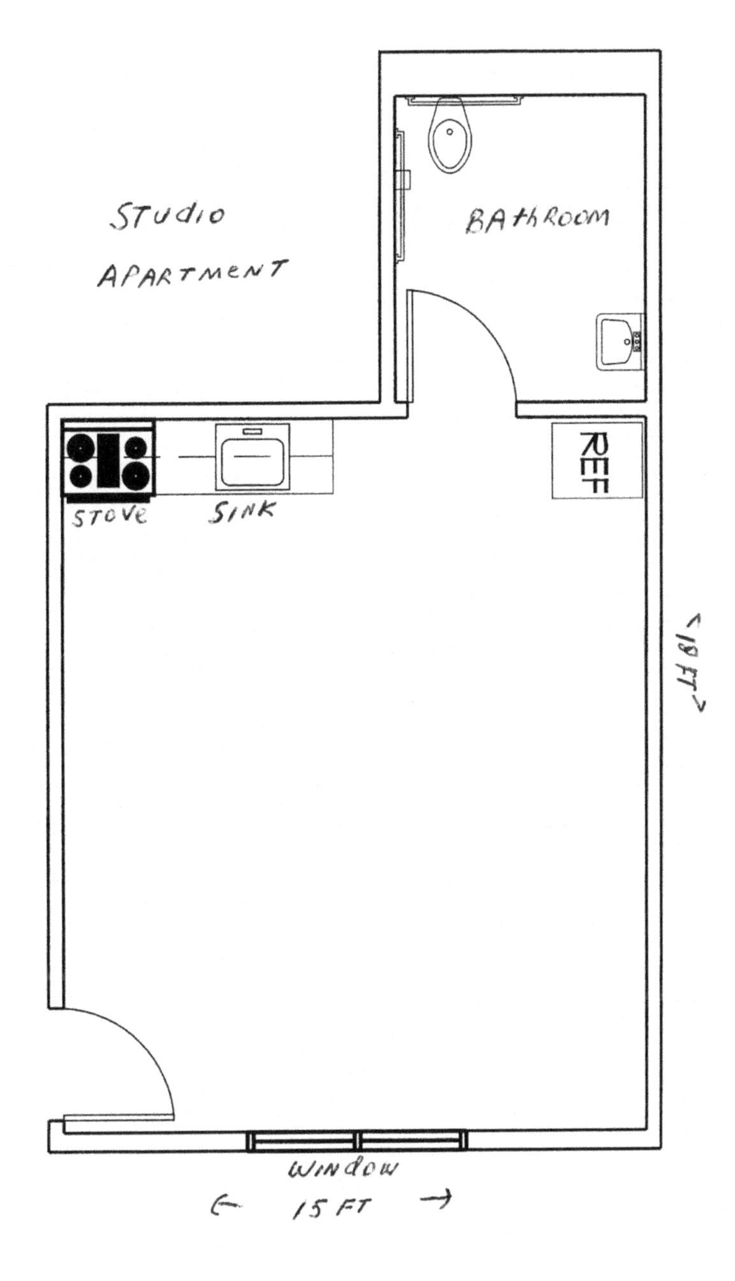

Writing Assignment 3

Describing Your Country

Because you were born in a foreign country, many Americans will ask you to describe your place of origin. They are curious to know about your native country. How would you describe your country to someone who knows very little about it? Explain the important places, physical features, the major cities and vacation places, and the people. Use an encyclopedia or an online source to fill in the information in the box.

Country	
Capital city	
Other major cities	
Rivers	
Lakes	
Mountains	
Population	
Religion(s)	
Size	
Places to visit	
Important products	
Major crops	
Main industries	
Language(s)	

Now use the information you have gathered to write a twelve-sentence paragraph about your country.

Writing Assignment 4

Reading and Writing

DEADWOOD, SOUTH DAKOTA

(1) When people think about the "Gold Rush," they usually picture California in 1849. Many people from the eastern United States traveled west to look for gold. When they think about the Wild West, they often get the idea of a small town in Nevada, Wyoming, or Colorado, with cowboys and cowgirls, sheriffs, and shootouts. However, there is one town that combined the two elements: gold found in the nearby Black Hills and a wild and crazy atmosphere in the town. It is Deadwood, South Dakota.

(2) In 1875, a miner named John B. Pearson found gold in a canyon in the Black Hills. This canyon became known as "Deadwood Gulch" because of the many dead trees that lined the canyon walls. The town of Deadwood began as a simple mining camp. Many tough people came from the east to make their fortunes. They wanted to find gold and become rich. After working in the mines, many came to the town of Deadwood to relax. There were many saloons with whiskey, dancing, and shows. There were so many gunfights that the town seemed lawless. Yet the people kept coming.

(3) Two of the most famous and colorful characters in Deadwood were Wild Bill Hickok and Calamity Jane. Hickok's legend was built on his ability to handle a pistol with either hand. He was the first of the so-called "fast guns." Most of his adult years were spent in the West: he worked for the Pony Express (the

western post office),and also as a detective and a scout in the U.S. Army. Wild Bill loved to gamble, and he died during a card game in Deadwood. He was shot in the back of the head by Jack McCall while playing poker at the No. 10 Saloon on August 2, 1876. He was holding two black aces, two black eights, and a five of diamonds. These cards are still known as "the dead man's hand."

(4) Calamity Jane was famous for her excellent marksmanship, her preference for men's clothing, and her bawdy behavior. While growing up in Montana in the far west, Jane developed skills that would make her reputation stronger: excellent horsemanship and marksmanship. She is said to have been drunk for most of her adult life. When not on the open road, Calamity Jane could be found at the Deadwood saloons drinking, chewing tobacco, and being the life of the party. She is buried in Mt. Moriah Cemetery in Deadwood, South Dakota. She was close to Wild Bill Hickok and her dying wish was to be buried next to him. And there she rests, a Deadwood legend.

(5) The houses in Deadwood in the 1870s were not typical western style. Many of them were Victorians, which makes the town unique in the West. They had beautiful front porches and high peaks. In September 1879, there was a great fire, and more than 300 buildings were destroyed. When the gold mine turned dry, many of the settlers left to look for treasure elsewhere. However, the city became a trading center for the Black Hills region when the railroad reached it in 1891.

(6) Today, Deadwood is fully restored. The whole city is on the National Historic Register. Deadwood's historic gaming halls date back to the Gold Rush of 1876. The action continues today in over eighty establishments. In November 1989, Deadwood became the third place in America to legalize gambling. The State of Nevada and Atlantic City, New Jersey, were the others. As the largest historic preservation project in the United States, Deadwood is a living showcase of history.

Exercise 1: Finding the main idea of a paragraph.
Match the paragraph number with its main idea.

___ Paragraph 1	a. The 1870s in Deadwood
___ Paragraph 2	b. Calamity Jane
___ Paragraph 3	c. Deadwood today
___ Paragraph 4	d. Wild Bill Hickok
___ Paragraph 5	e. Introduction to Deadwood
___ Paragraph 6	f. The beginnings of Deadwood

Exercise 2: Answer the questions in complete sentences. Use your own words.

1. Why did people first come to Deadwood?

2. Why do people come to Deadwood today?

3. How did Wild Bill Hickok die?

4. Why was Calamity Jane so famous?

5. Why are two black aces and two black 8s called "the dead man's hand"?

Exercise 3: Write a paragraph following the instructions provided.

1. Do you know any women (relative, friend, acquaintance, someone you read about) who are similar to Calamity Jane: strong, independent, and colorful? Write a paragraph in which you describe one of these extraordinary women.

2. Do you know any men (relative, friend, acquaintance, someone you read about) who are similar to Wild Bill Hickok, who has had many interesting jobs, but who has a wild nature and loves to do dangerous things? Write a paragraph in which you describe one of these extraordinary men.

Writing Assignment 5

Describing the Photograph

VACATION PLACES: OFF SEASON

Beach vacation places change completely on September 1. People no longer go swimming. The hotels and motels are mostly empty. The restaurants and bars have fewer customers. Even those people who make money from tourists—portrait painters, street performers, and tattoo artists—almost retire until the next season. There is a sense of sadness in the air.

Describe what is happening in the photograph. Tell where you think the young woman and artist are. What is the weather like? Is he a good artist? Does the portrait resemble the young woman? Is she happy or sad? What is she going to do with the portrait?

kavalenkava volha/Shutterstock.com

THE TRAVEL JOURNAL

When you travel, sometimes it is nice to keep a travel journal. You can present your impressions of the place and record the interesting things to do and see. You can write a travel journal on your vacations with your family, friends, or when you travel alone. In the next few weeks, write journal entries about the places that you visited on vacations in the past and also current trips.

During this semester, write a travel journal for all the places that you visit in America and also, using the past tense, add some descriptions of memorable vacations that you took before you came to this country. Here is an example of a travel journal entry.

Travel Journal
My European Vacation

June 5, 2007 Barcelona, Spain

It is early evening and I am sitting on the balcony of our hostel overlooking "Las Ramblas," a street packed with excitement day and night. Street performers are entertaining the people in the square for money. One man is wearing gold paint and standing so still he looks like a statue in a museum. Next to him, a young girl is dressed as a butterfly and is dancing gracefully as a large group of tourists surrounds her and takes pictures. Across the street an elderly couple is selling jewelry and singing loudly together to attract customers. I think we will go down to the square and eat a nice dinner outside. I can't wait to eat some more Paella Marina (Rice and Fish) and wash it down with a few glasses of Sangria (wine with fruit). The people here are so friendly, and I haven't seen one traffic jam yet like I see every day in America. I also heard that everyone in Spain takes a nap or "siesta" right in the middle of every day! Imagine that! I'm not sure I'll do that because I don't want to miss a minute of my stay in beautiful Barcelona.

Write a journal entry in which you describe a fun place that you visited on vacation.

____

____

____

____

____

____

____

____

THE DAY-TRIP LOG

Travel journals are not just for vacations, though. Maybe you don't have the money or the time to take a full vacation. You can use a travel journal to record ideas about "day trips." Some people love to get in the car and take a drive on their day off. They discover new and wonderful places. They eat in a good local restaurant and shop in the stores. They visit the tourist attractions, tour the old houses, and walk in beautiful parks. This is a nice way to refresh yourself and discover new places. Leave early in the morning and drive or take the bus to a place you have never visited before. Visit a natural place and take a walk in the mountains. Or go to a large city and enjoy the shops and the people. Drive to farm country and buy some fresh fruit and vegetables from a farm stand. Have fun looking at the animals.

Take pictures everywhere you go. Enjoy a day away from school and work. When you return, fill out the Day-Trip Log below. Try to take a short day-trip a few times during the semester. The following is an example of a day-trip log entry.

Day-Trip Log

Place: Pennsylvania Dutch Country (home of the Amish people)

Date visited: August 21, 2007

Time spent: 3 hours each way

Traveling companions: Gerard and Teddy

Means of transportation: Teddy's car, a 2002 Honda Civic

Things to see: The countryside is beautiful, with rolling hills and fields filled with plants. The houses are painted either white or red in the area. You can see the buggies that the Amish people drive because they do not drive cars. We saw a typical Amish house. They have no electricity and most of the things in the house are made of wood.

Interesting things to do: We took a tour of an Amish house and farm and saw many animals. We took pictures with cows and sheep. We walked on farm roads and visited several farm stands. We also rode in a buggy with two horses pulling it.

Where I ate (and what): Plain and Fancy Restaurant. All the tables are set for ten people, so you meet new people and eat with them. The food is served family style. They bring out big plates of ham, chicken, meat loaf, potatoes, and vegetables, and you take some and pass it to the other people at the table. The pies for dessert are fantastic. You have to practice you modals for polite requests. "Would you please pass the potatoes?" "Will you give me another piece of chicken?" "Would you mind passing the apple pie?"

Shopping: At the farm stands, you can buy really fresh vegetables and fruit. We also bought a few jars of homemade jelly.

Day-Trip Log

Place:

Date visited:
Time spent:
Traveling companion(s):

Means of transportation:

Nice things to see:

Interesting things to do:

Where you ate (and what):

Shopping:

People are fascinating. Because they are so diverse, they are a constant source of interest. Of course, famous people such as movie and television stars, musicians, singers, writers, professional athletes, and politicians always attract our attention. The magazines that tell their stories, with many photographs, sell millions of copies. In fact, *People, Us,* and *Entertainment Weekly* are among the best-selling publications in America.

We love to look at people. When we sit at an outside table at a restaurant or café, we concentrate on the people walking by. We certainly admire beauty. But we also focus on diversity. Does that man really have purple hair? Do you see her nose, lip, and tongue rings? What about that tattoo of the apple and the snake on his arm? Are those two really a couple? How did they end up together although they look so different? People-watching is a great activity. Later you describe the interesting people you have seen to your friends and family.

SUBJECT–VERB AGREEMENT

1. **Singular and plural subjects**
   The basic rule for subject and verb agreement is that *singular subjects take singular verbs and plural subjects take plural verbs.* In general, you will only notice these differences in the **present tense**. This is because in the past tense there is no difference between the singular and plural form of the verb. The only exception to this rule is the verb *to be*, which has a different singular (*was*) and a plural (*were*) form in the past. Let's examine a few examples.

   Bob (is / are) my brother's best friend.
   The new vice-president (come / comes) from Indiana.

   Should we use *is* or *are* in these sentences? Bob is singular, so we should use *is.* In the second sentence, there is only one new vice-president, so we must use *comes.*

   Nan and Barb (has / have) a special relationship.
   Sixteen teachers (works / work) at the new elementary school.

   In these sentences, Nan and Barb make a *plural* subject, so we should use the verb *have.* Sixteen teachers are also a *plural* subject, so we choose *work* as the correct verb form.

2. ***Each* and *every***

   The terms ***each*** and ***every*** are <u>always</u> followed by a <u>singular</u> verb. It doesn't matter if *each* and *every* are followed by one noun or a series of nouns; the singular verb is always used.

   Every student **has** to take the math test.
   Every man, woman, and child **is** protected by the law.
   Each part **is** sold separately.
   Each item on sale now **costs** only $5.

3. ***Some, a lot, most of,* and percents and fractions**

   Like *there*, the words ***some***, ***a lot***, and ***most of***, and **percentages** and **fractions** are either singular or plural depending on the noun that follows. Let's examine these examples:

   Some excellent wine **is** made in Chile.
   Some vegetables **grow** underground rather than above the ground.

   In the first sentence, *some* describes the word *wine*, which is non-count singular, so we use the singular verb *is*. The word *some* in the second sentences describes *vegetables*, which is plural. For this reason, we use the plural verb *grow*.

   A lot of the peaches in the basket **are** not ripe.
   A lot of the tea sold in America **comes** from India.
   Most of the managers at that company **work** on Saturdays.
   Most of the water in the river near the factory **is** polluted.

   To decide on what verb to use after *a lot* and *most of*, analyze the noun that follows. In the first sentence, the noun *peaches* is plural, so we use the plural verb *are*. *Tea* is singular (and non-count) in the second sentence, so the singular verb *comes* is used. In the third sentence, *managers* is plural, so we use *work*. In the last sentence, though, we choose the singular verb *is* because the noun *water* is non-count singular.

   Sixty percent of the students in the class **speak** three languages.
   Four-fifths of the spectators **are** cheering for the home team.
   Forty percent of the work **was** done by only five employees.
   One-half of the beer at the party **was** warm.

   For percents (e.g., 40 percent) and fractions (e.g., four-fifths), analyze the noun that follows the verb. In the first two sentences, the nouns *students* and *spectators* are plural, so the plural verbs *speak* and *are* are used. However, the nouns in the next two sentences, *work* and *beer*, are both non-count singular, so we use the singular verb *was* in both sentences.

4. **Blocks of money, distance, and time**
   Many times these blocks are considered singular.

   Fifty dollars is a lot to pay for one dinner.
   Five hundred miles is probably too far to drive in one day.
   Forty-five minutes is a very long coffee break.

5. **Special nouns**
   Some nouns are tricky. Study the following list and memorize the rule.

   Mathematics, statistics, economics, physics, aerobics
   Some academic subjects end in *-s*, but they are singular anyway.
   Mathematics **is** the most difficult subject for me. *Physics* **is** the easiest.

   Advice, news, and *hair* [on your head] are non-count singular.
   Her *advice* **was** perfect for the situation.
   The *news* **is** always bad because of the war.
   Karl's *hair* looks like a skunk.

   Police is plural. An individual (singular) is a *police officer.*
   The *police* **are** coming right away.
   A *police officer* sometimes **works** nights and weekends.

6. **Special construction: one of the (plural noun) + singular verb**
   In this structure, remember to use a singular verb because the subject is *one.*

   One of the **people** in the class **comes** from Vietnam.
   One of the **cars** in the garage **is** thirty years old.
   One of Matilda's **brothers is** a professional soccer player.

Exercise 1
Choose the correct form of the verb *to be* in parentheses.
1. Most of the workers in that company (comes / come) from the Chicago area.
2. Shara (has / have) six brothers.
3. My brother and I (spends / spend) a lot of money.
4. The team (is / are) very good.
5. Two hours (is / are) the perfect length for a movie.
6. Mr. Izaguerra and his sister (come / comes) from Venezuela.
7. My mother's advice (is / are) usually old-fashioned.
8. Six people (lives / live) in that small house.
9. Mathematics (is / are) very difficult for people with math phobia.
10. The police (makes / make) many arrests on Saturday night.
11. Every student in the class (speak / speaks) a different language.
12. One of my favorite meals (is / are) chicken and rice.

Exercise 2

Choose the correct form of the verb *to be* in parentheses.

1. Six miles (is / are) a long way to walk to school.
2. Louisa (has / have) two jobs.
3. Giovanni and Maria (has / have) a small apartment and three dogs.
4. The group (is / are) very large.
5. The jacket and the gloves (is / are) on the table.
6. Mr. Izaguerra (arrive / arrives) at work early every day.
7. The beer (is / are) very good.
8. Nine hundred dollars (is / are) a very high rent for that old building.
9. Mr. Iwasaki (dance / dances) very well.
10. Fifty percent of the book (is / are) about the vice-president.
11. Three fourths of the flowers in the garden (is / are) roses.
12. A lot of the information in that article (is / are) wrong.

Exercise 3

Correct the mistakes in the following sentences.

1. John work to much.
2. My sister never have time talk to me.
3. Sixteen miles take twenty minutes on the highway.
4. She never cry when she have an argument with she boyfriend.
5. His sisters comes home very late at night.
6. One of my friend are from India.
7. Her hair are long and blond.
8. The cheese are from Vermont.
9. My brother and my sister lives in big house.
10. Sixteen people in the class is from Asia.
11. He always go church Sunday.
12. In morning, Inez drink two cup coffee.
13. The professors at this college is nice, but they gives too many homeworks.
14. Physics are fascinating, but economics are too difficult for me.

The Writing Workout Page

INTERESTING PEOPLE

Some people have very strong characteristics. They may be negative or positive. Write brief descriptions of the following types of persons.

You have recently started a new company. You are very satisfied with the early success of the business. One of the main reasons you are so happy is your partner. Your partner has many excellent characteristics that make him or her easy to work with. Describe this person.	

There are some people that you just do not like. Their main characteristics are the opposite of what you respect and enjoy in another person. You are not comfortable with these people. You don't like to see them, talk to them, work with them, or sit beside them in class. Describe the type of people you can't stand.	

Many psychologists say that one of the most important aspects of a happy life is to have a good friend. What kind of person are they talking about? What are the principal personality traits of a good friend? Describe your best friend.	

Is there one relative whom you really do not like very much? It might be your Aunt Rosie, who is very cheap. Or else, it could be cousin Rudy, who always talks just about himself. Or maybe your brother-in-law, who thinks he is too good to talk to you. Describe your least favorite relative.	______ ______ ______ ______ ______ ______

Which person has taught you the most in life? Who has served as your "role model" (someone you try to imitate because of his or her excellent characteristics)? Describe the person you have learned the most from and also tell what you learned.	______ ______ ______ ______ ______ ______

PARTS OF SPEECH PRACTICE: ADJECTIVES

Adjectives are colorful words that describe nouns and pronouns. Adjectives are used in two positions in the sentence: either before the noun they modify or after a form of the verb *to be* (*am*, *is*, *are*, *was*, *were*, *will be*). In paragraphs of description, adjectives are the most important part of speech. They create clear pictures in our mind of precisely what the person, place, or object is like. Analyze the following sentences for grammar and syntax (word order):

The *tired* chef cooked a *terrible* meal. [*tired* goes before *chef* and *terrible* precedes *meal*]
She is *tall* and *slender*. [*tall* and *slender* follow the verb *to be* (*is*) and describe the pronoun *she*]
The *new* song was *romantic*. [*new* goes before the noun *song* and *romantic* follows the be-verb *was*]

Exercise on adjectives: Analyze the following photographs. Write four adjectives to describe the nouns presented. Share your adjectives with your classmates. Then write sentences using the adjectives.

© Brian Altano

____
____
____

© holbox/Shutterstock.com

____
____
____

© Brian Altano (author)

____
____
____

Writing Assignment 1

A Structural Approach

Read the following paragraph of description and follow the structure.

ANDREW, MY BROTHER

My favorite person in my family is my brother, Andrew. He is very funny. He tells excellent jokes all the time. He smiles and is always in a happy mood. In addition, he is a really good family member. He knows all the relatives on our complicated family tree. He even knows the brother-in-law of my grandmother's cousin. Andrew is also hard working. He works many hours. In work, he is very patient and he wants to do a perfect job. I really love my younger brother Andrew.

Exercise on Adjectives: Underline or highlight all the adjectives in the paragraph. Write them in the spaces below:

1. ______	2. ______	3. ______
4. ______	5. ______	6. ______
7. ______	8. ______	9. ______
10. ______	11. ______	12. ______
13. ______	14. ______	15. ______

The description paragraph about Andrew has eleven sentences. Here is a list of how each sentence functions.

The Structure of the Paragraph

Sentence 1: Topic sentence (name of the person)

My favorite person in my family is my brother, Andrew.

Sentence 2: First characteristic

He is very funny.

Sentence 3: Support (why? how?)

He tells excellent jokes all the time.

Sentence 4: Support (example)

He smiles and is always in a happy mood.

Sentence 5: Second characteristic

In addition, he is a really good family member.

Sentence 6: Support (why? how?)

He knows all the relatives on our complicated family tree.

Sentence 7: Support (example)

He even knows the brother-in-law of my grandmother's cousin.

Sentence 8: Third characteristic

Andrew is also hard working.

Sentence 9: Support (why? how?)

He works many hours.

Sentence 10: Support (example)

In work, he is very patient and he wants to do a perfect job.

Sentence 11: Conclusion

I really love my younger brother Andrew.

Writing Assignment 2

Description of a Family Member

In every family there is at least one person who is very interesting. It might be your grandfather, who tells stories and jokes and keeps everyone laughing. It might be your aunt, who has had many different and interesting jobs. Maybe it is your sister, who has been married four times.

In a clearly written paragraph describe the most interesting person in your family. Tell why the person is so interesting. You might write about the person's personality and anything he or she has done in life.

Use an eleven-sentence structure. Also use the paragraph about Andrew as a model to write a paragraph describing the most interesting person in your family.

Verb tense: simple present tense
Structure: At least **THREE** characteristics, with one or two supporting sentences for each one. For example:

My brother is very generous.
[This sentence presents a characteristic.]
Every time we go to a restaurant or to the movies, he pays.
[This is a supporting sentence. It tells how he is generous.]

The characteristics may be PHYSICAL. (*He is tall and thin.*)

The characteristics might describe his or her PERSONALITY. (*She is very friendly and outgoing.*)

Use *spatial organization* (as you did for describing places). Move from top to bottom in your physical description, and then from outside to inside to describe a person physically and then in terms of personality and nature.

Writing Assignment 3

Description of the Photograph

Write a biography of the woman in the photograph. Describe the many aspects of her life. Use the past tense to talk about the events that have led to her current condition. Also describe her at present.

Writing Assignment 4

A Strong and Powerful Woman

Who is the most powerful woman in your family?

Write a short biography of the matriarch (*arch* = power, government; *matri* = mother) of your clan.

Verb tense: simple present tense
Structure: At least **THREE** characteristics, with one or two supporting sentences for each one. Make sure that you explain how this strong woman is a leader in your family. Include a copy of a photograph with your paragraph, if you have one.

Writing Assignment 5

Description Paragraphs: A Step-by-Step Process

MY BEST TEACHER

You are going to write a description paragraph using a step-by-step process. This process involves three steps:

1. **Pre-writing**: Choose a topic, brainstorm characteristics, and narrow the list.
2. **Outlining**: Prepare an idea cluster.
3. **Writing**: Follow the idea cluster to write your paragraph.

1. **Choose a topic, brainstorm characteristics, and narrow the list:**
   a. First, choose a topic. For this assignment, you will write about ***the best teacher*** that you have ever had.
   My Best Teacher, ______________________

   b. Now, think about the strongest characteristics of this person. Write down up to eight of them. This process is called *brainstorming*.

   ______________________ ______________________

   ______________________ ______________________

   ______________________ ______________________

   ______________________ ______________________

   c. Read over the list. You will not need so many characteristics for your paragraph. You should narrow the list. Choose the best four. Write them below:

   ______________________ ______________________

   ______________________ ______________________

2. **Prepare an Idea Cluster**

   Filling out an idea cluster is an excellent way to organize your thoughts in description writing. (Following is an idea cluster example.)

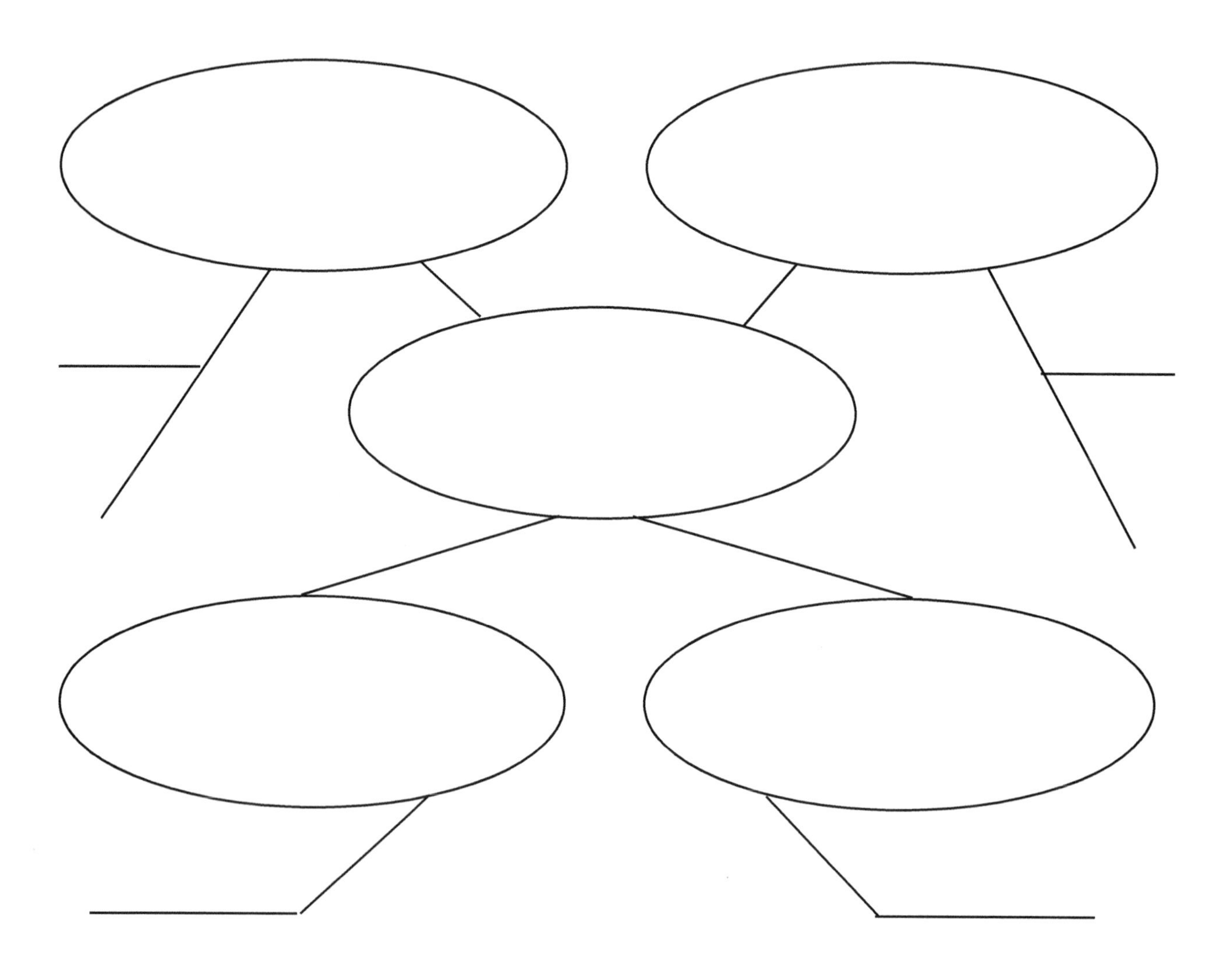

Follow these steps to fill out the idea cluster

1. In the center oval, write the topic.
2. In the oval on the bottom right, write a characteristic.
3. Start at the edge of the oval. Draw a line. On the line, write notes to support the characteristic.
4. Draw another line from that line. Write notes to support the information you wrote on the line. This might be an example or additional information.
5. In the oval on the top right, write another characteristic.
6. Start at the edge of the oval. Draw a line. On the line, write notes to support the characteristic.
7. Draw another line from that line. Write notes to support the information you wrote on the line. This might be an example or additional information.
8. In the oval on the top left, write the third characteristic.
9. Start at the edge of the oval. Draw a line. On the line, write notes to support the characteristic.
10. Draw another line from that line. Write notes to support the information you wrote on the line. This might be an example or additional information.
11. In the oval on the bottom left, write the fourth (last) characteristic.
12. Start at the edge of the oval. Draw a line. On the line, write notes to support the characteristic.
13. Draw another line from that line. Write notes to support the information you wrote on the line. This might be an example or additional information.

3. **Follow the idea cluster to write your paragraph.**
   When the idea cluster is complete, you will be ready to write an organized paragraph.

THE MOST INTERESTING PERSON IN MY FAMILY

The most interesting person in my family is Beatrice. She is my great aunt, my grandmother's sister. She has many interesting characteristics. First, she is very ugly. She has a big nose and a thick moustache. In fact, she was the person who taught me how to shave when I was 16. Another characteristic is that she is very generous. Beatrice gave me an allowance of $25 per month for more than 30 years. The third characteristic is that she is a smart shopper. She lived next to a supermarket, and went there every day. She used coupons, and saved a lot of money. Finally, Beatrice is a hard-worker. She worked 60 years at the same job. She didn't retire until she was 75. She still cooks and cleans by herself. These are the reasons why I think Beatrice is the most interesting person in my family.

MUHAMMAD ALI

The person I admire most is Muhammad Ali. Ali was born with the name Cassius Clay in 1942 in Louisville, Kentucky. When he was 18 years old, he won the gold medal as light heavyweight champion at the 1960 Olympics in Rome, Italy. He won his first professional championship in 1964 when he knocked out Sonny Liston. Soon after he became the champion, he adopted the Muslim religion and changed his name to Muhammad Ali. Ali was a great boxer. He was very fast and intelligent. He was fearless, too. Most of all, he was very confident. He always believed that he was going to win. Ali was an excellent fighter, but he was even more important as a political person. When he was called into the army during the Vietnam War, Ali refused to go. Because of his strong religious beliefs, he was against war and killing. The military officials said that if he did not join the army, they would take away his title as heavyweight champion of the world. And so it happened. He did not box for three and a half years. In 1971, the Supreme Court reversed Ali's conviction, and he was allowed to fight again. He won the championship again. His greatest fights were against Joe Frazier and George Foreman. I admire Muhammad Ali for his courage. He gave up his title because of his beliefs. He was not afraid to speak out against the war and about racial problems in the United States. Now, many people respect and love Ali. At the beginning of the 1996 Olympics in Atlanta, Georgia, Muhammad Ali was chosen to light the Olympic torch, the symbol of peace.

Answer the following questions. Use your own words:

1. When was Muhammad Ali born? ______________________________

2. Where was he born? ______________________________

3. What happened to him in 1960? ______________________________

4. In boxing, what happened to Ali in 1964? ______________________________

   ____

5. What else did Ali do in 1964? ______________________________

6. Why didn't Ali go into the U.S. army to fight in the Vietnam war? ______________________________

   ____

7. What did the military officials do? ______________________________

8. What happened to him in 1971? ______________________________

9. Why does the writer admire Ali? ______________________________

   ____

10. What did Muhammad Ali do at the 1996 Olympics in Atlanta, Georgia? ____________________

____

Highlight all the adjectives in the passage and copy them in the spaces below.

____________	____________	____________	____________
____________	____________	____________	____________
____________	____________	____________	____________
____________	____________	____________	____________

THE PERSON I ADMIRE MOST

In this paragraph, you will describe the person you admire most, the one you think deserves the most respect.

Tell why you admire the person. Introduce his or her best characteristics and tell what the person has done in life to deserve your admiration. The person may be a family member (mother, father, brother, sister, aunt, etc.), a major political figure (president, prime minister, king, queen, governor, mayor), a sport figure, entertainer, writer, teacher, or a religious figure (priest, minister, rabbi, imam, guru).

If the person you admire is famous, you might have to conduct research. You want to find out details about his or her life. In the space below, write notes about the person's life.

Person I admire most: ____________________

Description: ____________________

____

____

Significant actions: ____________________

____

____

Why you admire him/her: ____________________

____

____

Writing Assignment 6

In-Class Activity

Time:	60 minutes
Pre-writing:	Take notes and make an idea cluster to help you organize your work.
Verb tenses:	**Simple present** for the description; **simple past** to tell about the significant actions that this person has performed.
Organization:	Present characteristics of the person and then tell why you respect and admire him or her.
Topic sentence:	Probably a simple one such as "Michael Jordan is the person I admire most" would work well.
Writing:	Write on a separate sheet of paper. This assignment will be handed in at the end of the class. Write on every other line. (Write on one line and then skip a line.) Write nine to twelve sentences.

DESCRIPTION OF THE PERFECT SPOUSE

Using the simple present tense, describe the PERFECT SPOUSE (husband, wife) or the PERFECT GIRLFRIEND/BOYFRIEND. What characteristics does this person have?

Use he is / she is; he has / she has; etc.
Do <u>not</u> use future or modals. Pretend that the person is real. **Use the simple present tense.**

1. List up to eight characteristics of the perfect spouse.

_______________ _______________

_______________ _______________

_______________ _______________

_______________ _______________

2. Read over the list. You will not need so many characteristics for your paragraph. You should narrow the list. Choose the best four. Write them here:

_______________ _______________

_______________ _______________

3. Prepare an idea cluster, and then follow the cluster to write your paragraph.

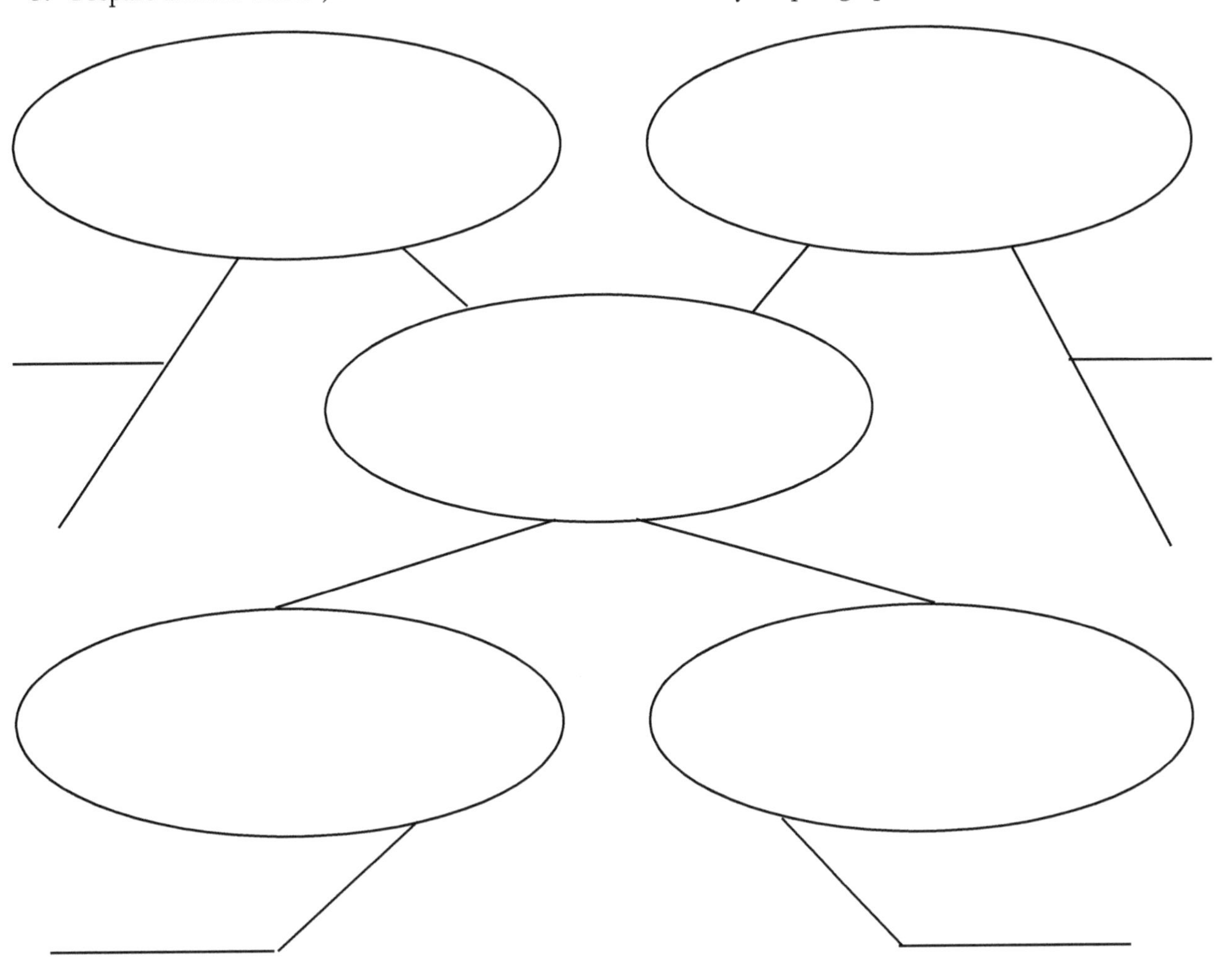

THE INTERESTING PERSON JOURNAL

You read about them all the time. You see them on television and hear about them on the radio. You find them on the internet. You wish you could meet them. We are fascinated by famous people. However, some of the people we meet every day are also intriguing. They have mysterious histories, attractive personalities, and curious physical and emotional characteristics. In fact, interesting people make life so enjoyable.

For the next two weeks write an "interesting people" journal. Concentrate on a different person each day. You may write about famous people or just regular, simple people who you meet in your everyday life. Describe them and tell what you find fascinating about them. Choose people living today as well as some who lived in the past. The following is a sample journal entry about a famous man living today.

BARACK OBAMA

(1) Barack Hussein Obama Jr. is the forty-fourth U.S. president, the first African American president, and the first president born in Hawaii. Obama was born on August 4, 1961, in Honolulu, Hawaii. His mother, Ann Dunham, is from Kansas. Obama's father, Barack Obama Sr., comes from Kenya, Africa. His parents met when Obama Sr. was on a scholarship at the University of Hawaii and Ann Dunham was studying there. They married on February 2, 1961, and Barack Jr. was born six months later in Hawaii. They divorced in 1964, and Obama Sr. returned to Africa in 1965. Obama Jr.'s mother remarried to an Indonesian student , Lolo Saetoro, also studying in Hawaii. When he was recalled to Indonesia in 1967, Ann Dunham, Obama Jr., and his half-sister, moved to Indonesia. From age 6 to 10, Obama went to school in Jakarta, Indonesia. In 1971, Obama returned to Hawaii to live with his maternal grandparents.

(2) President Obama graduated from Columbia University in New York in 1983 with a major in political science. He then entered law school and earned a degree from Harvard University Law School in 1991. He was president of the *Harvard Law Review*, the oldest operating law journal in America edited by students. He gained a national reputation as the first African American president of the *Law Review* and earned a book contract to write an autobiography. The book, *Dreams from My Father*, was published in 1995.

(3) After he earned his law degree, Obama worked as a civil rights attorney in Chicago at Davis, Miner, Barnhill & Galland, a law firm of twelve attorneys specializing in civil rights litigation and neighborhood economic development. He also taught constitutional law from 1992 to 2004 at the University of Chicago Law School. At this time, he also visited his relatives in Kenya, a trip that included a stop at the grave sites of his biological father and his paternal grandfather.

(4) Obama entered politics in 1997, at the age of 36. He served three terms in the Illinois Senate (1997–2004). In 2000, he lost the election for House of Representatives from Illinois. In July 2004, Obama wrote and delivered the keynote address at the 2004 Democratic National Convention, which was held in Boston, Massachusetts. His speech was seen by 9 million people and was one of the highlights of the convention. He became broadly known around the country, and it raised his status in the Democratic policy. Just a few months later, in November 2004, Obama won the election as Senator from Illinois, winning 70 percent of the vote.

(5) In November 2008, only four years later, he won the election for president against Senator John McCain. He won 53 percent of the vote, compared to 46 percent for McCain. In the electoral vote, Obama won 365 to 173. On January 20, 2009, he became president of the United States. At age 47, Obama was the fifth youngest man to become president (after Theodore Roosevelt, John F. Kennedy, Bill Clinton, and Ulysses Grant). Obama is married to Michelle Robinson Obama, an attorney, whom he wed in 1992. The couple has two daughters, Malia Ann, born in 1998, and Natasha ("Sasha"), born in 2001.

(6) On October 9, 2009, President Obama was awarded the Nobel Peace Prize "for his extraordinary efforts to strengthen international diplomacy and cooperation between peoples." As specific examples of the work that led to the award, the Nobel Prize Committee highlighted his efforts to promote nuclear non-proliferation (especially in Iran), and the fostering of a "new climate" in international relations, especially in reaching out to the Muslim world. He was reelected in 2012 with a strong majority of the votes.

Choose the correct answer:

1. President Obama studied for six years in Indonesia when he was young.
   a. true b. false
2. President Obama's biological father comes from Indonesia.
   a. true b. false
3. President Obama's mother studied at the University of Hawaii.
   a. true b. false
4. President Obama's stepfather studied at the University of Hawaii.
   a. true b. false
5. President Obama lived with his grandparents before 1971.
   a. true b. false
6. President Obama's mother married three times.
   a. true b. false
7. President Obama studied law at Columbia.
   a. true b. false
8. President Obama's first book was an autobiography.
   a. true b. false
9. President Obama became a senator from Hawaii in 2004.
   a. true b. false
10. Obama never practiced law. Instead, he became a politician immediately after law school.
    a. true b. false
11. How many presidents have been born in Hawaii?
    a. one b. two c. three d. four
12. How many African American presidents have there been?
    a. one b. two c. three d. four
13. How many presidents were younger than Obama?
    a. one b. two c. three d. four
14. The president is named Barack Obama, Jr. because:
    a. his father comes from Kenya. b. he was born in Hawaii.
    c. he is African American. d. he has the same name as his father.
15. We can infer from paragraph 1 that in 1971:
    a. he went to live in Kenya. b. his parents returned with him to Hawaii.
    c. he remained in Indonesia. d. he returned without his parents to Hawaii.

Writing Assignment 7

Journal Activity

Make photocopies of this page or use the format to describe a different interesting person every day for the next two weeks.

The Interesting Person Journal

Name:

Date of birth / age: (if living now)

Date of birth / death: (if the person lived in the past)

Nationality:

Description:

Achievements:

Why do you find the person so interesting?

Objects sometimes have special significance. In this way, an object that may not be worth much in cash, has vast sentimental value. For example, a watch that your grandfather gave you on your tenth birthday is worth so much to you because it reminds you of him. The same is true with a letter from your brother when he was in the army and photographs of you and your friends living far away. This is why if these objects are lost or stolen, they are irreplaceable.

Our senses are also linked to memory. A particular perfume may remind you of your mother. The aroma of spices cooking slowly in a soup recalls the restaurant on the corner from where you used to live. The taste of chocolate brings back your afternoon snack when you went to elementary school. The music from an old song reminds you of your first date. The touch of a baseball glove brings back memories of games played in Little League. The sight of a vivid color calls to mind a special party dress that you wore when you were a teenager.

Grammar in Context

COMPLETE SENTENCES AND SENTENCE FRAGMENTS

The basic structure in language is the sentence. A sentence is composed of at least two elements: a subject and a verb. Of course, there may be other parts of speech used in addition to the subject and verb. A complete sentence, though, must have at least one subject and one verb, and it must express a complete idea. Let's examine the following:

The tiny, smooth, shiny white mouse

Is this group of words a complete sentence? Look closely. Find a noun. There it is: the word *mouse.* Mouse is the subject of the sentence. Now look for a verb. None of the other words in the group is a verb. No verb? No complete sentence. Now let's examine another group of words.

smiled happily at everyone at the dinner table.

Is this group of words a complete sentence? In this group, we find a verb: *smiled.* Who smiled? We don't know because there is no subject. No subject? No complete sentence.
Let's analyze another group of words.

Nigel died.

Here we have only two words. The word groups in the first two examples had six and eight words but were not complete sentences. Is *Nigel died* a complete sentence? Well, **Nigel** is a noun and serves as the subject; **died** is a verb. So we have both a subject and a verb. The words express a complete idea. Therefore, *Nigel died* is a complete sentence.

Let's look at a few more word groups:

1. Joe left his coffee cup on top of the car.
2. spilled her drink all over the new white rug
3. The man with the tattoo of two snakes
4. in the afternoon after the end of the difficult French examination
5. The pilot chewed her fingernails during the terrible storm.

Which ones are complete sentences? In number one, **Joe** is the subject and **left** is the verb. This makes a complete sentence. In the second sentence, **spilled** is the verb, but *who* spilled the drink? We don't know because there is no subject. Number two is incomplete. In grammar language, an incomplete sentence is called a sentence fragment. In sentence number three, we have a subject, *the man*, but no verb. This is also a fragment. In the fourth sentence, we have three prepositional phrases (*in the afternoon, after the end, of the difficult French examination*). However, we have *no subject* and *no verb*. Number four is also a sentence fragment. The last sentence has a subject (the pilot) and a verb, and expresses a complete idea. For this reason, it is a complete sentence. Thus, the only two complete sentences are the first one and the last one.

Incomplete Ideas

Sometimes a clause has a subject and a verb, but it is still not a complete sentence because it does not present a complete idea. Let's take a look at these examples:

Carla loves
Wan Bo is buying
The teacher explained

In these three examples, we need *objects* to make complete sentences. What (or whom) does Carla love? What is Wan Bo buying? What did the teacher explain? We must add more information to make a complete sentence:

Carla loves cold pizza.	Carla loves Jim.
Wan Bo is buying a new wig.	Wan Bo is buying the grammar textbook.
The teacher explained the answer.	The teacher explained dependent clauses.

Independent Clauses

A subject and verb taken together form a clause. When a clause forms a complete idea and can stand by itself, it is called an **independent clause.** In order to form a complete sentence, there must be at least one independent clause.

Clauses beginning with coordinating conjunctions—dependent clauses

A dependent clause has a subject and a verb. However, it begins with a coordinating conjunction so it cannot stand alone. It is not a complete sentence. Let's analyze the following example.

Barbara wrote a long paragraph.

This is an independent clause and a complete sentence. We place a period at the end. Now we will add a coordinating conjunction at the beginning of the clause:

After Barbara wrote a long paragraph

The addition of the conjunction **after** changes the clause from independent to *dependent*. We are waiting for more information, so it is incomplete. In order to make a complete sentence, we must add an *independent clause:*

After Barbara wrote a long paragraph, she went for a walk.

Now we have a complete sentence. Whenever a clause begins with a coordinating conjunction, it will be a dependent clause and an incomplete sentence. Examine the following examples:

1. If you love me, you will let my mother stay with us for a month.
2. Because it is raining, we cannot have a picnic.
3. When she saw her ex-boyfriend, Carol became angry.
4. Although Wiemer has a lot of money, he doesn't have any friends.
5. Ms. Witherspoon sold the house after her father died.
6. Yao studied extra vocabulary because he wanted to get a good grade.

In the first four examples, the sentence begins with a dependent clause. The second clause (an independent clause) is necessary to form a complete sentence. The last two sentences show that the dependent clause may also go in the middle of the sentence.

Exercise 1: Complete and incomplete sentences

Write F next to a sentence fragment and explain why it is so (no subject, no verb, not a complete idea). Write C next to complete sentences.

1. ___ Nestor shaved his back ____________________
2. ___ When I see her ____________________
3. ___ Loves to read in the kitchen ____________________
4. ___ Macey likes to look out the window. ____________________
5. ___ If you really need my help ____________________

6. ___ The nurse helped the sick doctor ______________________

7. ___ The incredibly large scar on his nose ______________________

8. ___ Is a beautiful day today. ______________________

9. ___ The dog barked all night long. ______________________

10. ___ Because the sun is so hot ______________________

11. ___ Every day, go to work early ______________________

12. ___ After the very exciting game ______________________

13. ___ Before lunch, Hanna worked out ______________________

14. ___ Never in my whole life ______________________

15. ___ Nancy loves ______________________

Exercise 2: Independent and dependent clauses

Place a period after an independent clause. Place a comma after a dependent clause and complete the sentence by adding an independent clause. If the idea is not complete, add words to complete it. The first two are done for you.

1. After she got home from work, ***Gertrude ate a delicious dinner.***
2. I never cook on Sundays**(.)** **[independent clause]**
3. When Kristie walked into the room ______________________
4. If you need a little money ______________________
5. Mark loves ______________________
6. Before Rita left for the movies ______________________
7. Othelia is a very happy woman ______________________
8. Robert hates ______________________
9. Because Lester is so lazy ______________________
10. It rained all day and all night ______________________
11. The doctor explained ______________________
12. I always wash the dishes ______________________
13. Although Pat studied hard ______________________
14. This computer is very fast ______________________
15. After I watched the late-night news ______________________

Writing Assignment 1

Describing Objects

GIVING GIFTS

When you want to give an excellent gift, you should think of other people. What is their favorite color? Do they like casual or elegant clothes? What kind of music do they listen to? What kind of books do they like to read? What kind of sports do they play? Do they like to watch DVDs? Do they cook and have dinner parties? Do they enjoy walking in the woods or in a park? Dancing? Watching films? Bowling?

Write down the gifts that you will give on the following occasions. Try to write noun phrases (article + adjective + noun). For example:

a gold watch | *an exciting new movie* | *a short black skirt*
a French cookbook | *a mystery novel* | *a pair of jogging sneakers*

OCCASION	GIFT
Your best friend's birthday	
Your cousin's wedding	
Your mother on mother's day	
The letter carrier at the end of the year	
Your younger brother on his high school graduation	
Your younger sister on her sixteenth birthday (sweet sixteen)	
Your friend for her baby shower	
Your partner on Valentine's Day	
Your father on father's day	
Your boss when you are invited to her house for dinner	

Now write a ten-sentence paragraph describing the best gift that you ever gave someone. Tell when you gave it, who you gave it to, and on what occasion. Then explain how you felt when you gave this special gift.

Writing Assignment 2

Description of Your Most Prized Possession

Suppose that there is a fire in your house. You have time to save only one thing. This thing would probably be your most important (prized) possession. This possession has special significance for you. Perhaps it is valuable, such as a diamond ring or a gold watch. Perhaps its value is more sentimental. It may be a diary that you kept when you were fifteen years old, or the box from your first chocolate heart that you received on Valentine's Day four years ago. It might be a letter from your school principal telling you that you won the writing contest, or a photograph of you and your best friend from the first grade.

In a clearly written, well-organized paragraph, describe your most important possession. After you describe it completely, tell why it is so important to you.

© Brian J. Altano

The Writing Workout Page

MYSTERY OBJECTS

Read the following paragraphs and try to figure out the unnamed mystery object.

You use them in the house. You never wear them outside. Some people only put them on after they take a bath or shower. Others wear them in the house all the time. They are usually soft and warm. They are very comfortable. Both children and adults wear them. You wear them on your feet.

Mystery object: ____________________

You use this thing after you take a shower. You primarily use it in the bathroom. Some people wear it when they walk from the bathroom to the bedroom, before they get dressed. Many of them are white, but you may find them in all colors. They are soft and they absorb water very well.

Mystery object: ____________________

You use this in the kitchen. You put food in it to make it hot. You can also heat up drinks in it. Many of them have a digital clock. To use it, you push a few buttons and then Start. It makes a strange noise while it is working and it beeps when it is finished. It is an excellent place to make popcorn.

Mystery object: ____________________

You use this to talk to your friends and family. You carry it in your pocket or your bag. It sometimes rings at the wrong time, such as in class or at the movies. You can also use this as a camera or to tell time. You pay for this item with a monthly bill. You can use this thing almost everywhere, in the street, at home, at the mall, or in your car.

Mystery object: ____________________

You can find this object in two materials: silk or wool. The wool object is used in the winter when it is very cold. You can use the silk object all year round. Women usually use the silk object. Both men and women use the wool one. The silk object is almost always very elegant. Famous designers put their names on the silk objects. People wear both the silk and the wool objects around their necks. They wrap them around once or twice.

Mystery object: ____________________

When you are driving, you use this to look behind you and see other cars. Some people use this to check out their own hair and face. This item has to be adjusted according to the height of the driver. The outside is made of plastic, and the inside is made of special glass.

Mystery object: ____________________

Writing Assignment 3

Writing Descriptions of Mystery Objects

Using the previous five paragraphs about mystery objects as models, try to write six- or seven-sentence paragraphs. Describe the object, but don't name it. Write *three* different paragraphs.

Paragraph 1

Paragraph 2

Paragraph 3

1. Bring your paragraphs to class.
2. Exchange books (or papers if you write on separate sheets) with a partner.
3. Read your partner's paragraphs and try to guess the mystery objects.
4. Discuss the paragraphs with your partner.
5. Exchange paragraphs with a different partner and read his or her paragraphs. Try to guess the mystery objects.
6. You might also read one of your paragraphs aloud. The class will try to guess the mystery objects.

Writing Assignment 4

Your Favorite Toys

Describe your favorite toys when you were a child. What toys did you love to play with? Did you like action figures? Did you play with dolls? How about video games? Did you build houses with blocks? Or did you prefer to draw pictures with crayons or paint?

© Brian J. Altano

Writing Assignment 5

Description of Activities

Verb Tense:	**Simple Present**
Organization:	Activities in the cafeteria, moving around the room in an organized manner (left to right, front of the room to back of the room, etc.)
Grammar Points:	Quantity words Some people (are) Other people (are) Others (are) Some students (are) Several students (are) A few students (are) One student (is)

1. Go to the cafeteria and observe the activities of the students and workers.
2. Write down a list of SUBJECTS and VERBS (e.g., cook/prepares; students/talk; professor/eats).
3. You are going to write in the SIMPLE PRESENT TENSE.
4. Your topic sentence will be something like:
   EVERY DAY THE B.C.C. CAFETERIA IS FULL OF ACTIVITY.

Write ten to twelve sentences describing activities in the cafeteria. Use the simple present tense.

Writing Assignment 6

Scary Fun

Many people enjoy doing dangerous activities for fun. They like to go mountain climbing, whitewater rafting, or dirtbike riding. Even when they relax and go to an amusement park, some people love to ride thrilling roller coasters. They do not mind riding upside-down and traveling eighty miles an hour.

Do you like to have scary fun? Is doing dangerous activities attractive to you? If not, explain why you do not prefer these activities. Also, if you do not enjoy extreme activities, do you know people who do? Why do you think they like to do these things so much?

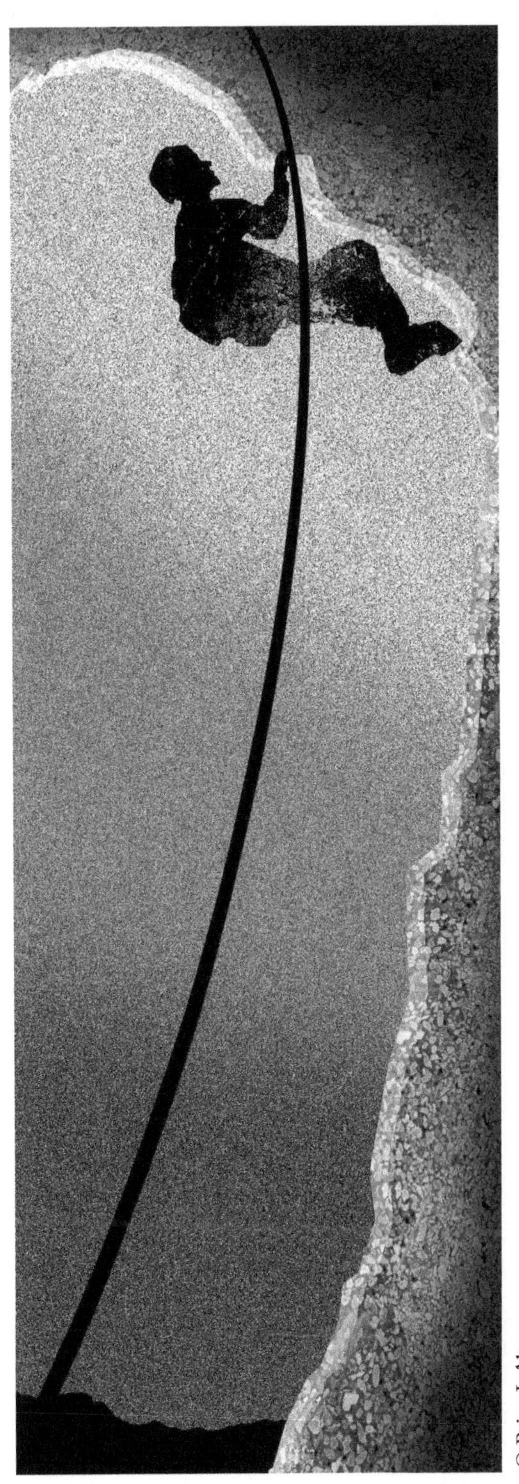

Writing Assignment 7

FAVORITES AND LEAST FAVORITES

Fill in the chart, listing your favorites and least favorites for the following categories.

ITEM	FAVORITE	LEAST FAVORITE
Color		
Time of the day		
Day of the week		
Month of the year		
Season		
Sport		
Team		
Athlete		
Soap		
Shampoo		
Cologne		
Singer		
Song		
Actress		
Actor		
Movie		
Television program		
Room of the house		
City		

Food		
Type of music		
Writer		
Relative		
Chore around the house		
Aroma		
Taste		
Things to touch		
Sounds		
Things to look at		

1. Working in groups of four, discuss your choices. Cite examples and try to give reasons why you prefer your responses.
2. Concentrate on the last five answers on the chart. These responses focus on the five senses (sight, hearing, smell, touch, and taste). Write a paragraph in which you describe pleasant sensory experiences. Cite specific examples to support your choices.
3. Again focus on the last five responses. This time, though, work from the negative point of view, and describe the five most unpleasant sensory experiences.
4. Choose other responses in the chart to write short paragraphs or journal entries.

Writing Assignment 8

Eating Habits

DESCRIBING YOUR EATING HABITS

Paragraph:	Describing Your Eating Habits
Verb tense:	Simple present
Organization:	According to meals and snacks
Grammar point:	Use adverbs of frequency (see below)
Constructions:	Prepositional phrases such as *for breakfast*, *for lunch*, and *for dinner* may be used at the beginning or at the end of the sentence: *For breakfast*, I usually eat ... I often eat [...] *for lunch.* I never eat [...] *for dinner.* *On the weekends*, I occasionally drink ... I always drink ... *on Saturday night.*
Vocabulary:	*meals and food*: breakfast, lunch, dinner, supper, snack, junk food *adjectives*: spicy, delicious, bland (flavorless), flavorful, hot, quick, healthy *verbs*: drink, eat, have (coffee, dinner), cook, prepare, serve, snack

Grammar Point: Adverbs of frequency

When you describe your eating habits, you will use adverbs of frequency to tell how often you eat and drink certain items. Study the list below and try to use these adverbs in your writing:

100%	always
90%	almost always
80%	usually
70%	frequently
60%	often
50%	sometimes
40%	occasionally
30%	rarely
20%	seldom
10%	almost never
0%	never

Placing the Adverbs of Frequency in the Sentence:

1. Adverbs of frequency are placed **after** the subject and **before** the verb. Analyze the following examples:

   I always buy a sandwich for lunch.
   Sally often has a cup of coffee at 3:00 p.m.
   Nancy occasionally eats a bagel for breakfast.
   Sheldon rarely drinks tea.
   Mustafa never eats pork.

2. Adverbs of frequency are placed **after a be-verb** (*am, is, are, was, were*). In the future, the adverb is placed **between** *will* and the base form verb.

   ***I am never** late.*
   *Nestor **is often** nervous when he takes a test.*
   *The boss **is frequently** angry at John and Joe.*
   *Your sister **will always be** there for you.*

3. **Sometimes** may be used in three positions in the sentence.
   a. at the beginning of the sentence: *Sometimes I drink coke or seven-up.*
   b. after the subject and before the verb: *Michael sometimes makes a hot breakfast.*
   c. at the end of the sentence: *Sidney eats alone sometimes.*

Fill out the information in the chart.

Meal	Food you often eat	Drinks	Food you never or almost never eat
Breakfast			
Lunch			
Dinner (supper)			
Snacks			

Writing assignment: In a twelve-sentence paragraph, describe your eating habits. Tell what you eat for breakfast, lunch, dinner, and for snacks. Also, include what you usually drink during the day. Indicate if you eat differently on the weekends. Add sentences telling what you never drink or eat.

CARBOHYDRATES: GOOD OR BAD FOR YOU?

It is January 2005. Robert Jackson and Henry Jefferson are sitting at their favorite diner for lunch. They usually eat lunch together on Thursdays. Both are a little overweight. Henry orders a chicken sandwich on a roll. "No oil, butter, or mayonnaise, please. Make sure it's grilled, not fried. And give me a fruit salad and a glass of milk." Robert orders a huge half-pound hamburger, but with no bun. "Wrap it in a lettuce leaf," he tells the waitperson. The waitperson patiently writes down the order. She is accustomed to dieters and their special needs. Both men are on a diet, but they are eating completely different meals.

Henry is following the traditional food pyramid designed by the United States Department of Agriculture (USDA) in the 1960s (see diagram). The USDA identified five major food groups: (1) milk, yogurt, cheese; (2) meat, fish, poultry, eggs, and nuts; (3) vegetables; (4) fruit; (5) bread, cereal, rice, and pasta. The diet is balanced. People are recommended to eat two to three servings from the dairy group, two to three servings from the meat group, three to five servings from the vegetable group, two to four servings from the fruit group, and eight to eleven servings from the grain group every day. At the very top of the pyramid is the fat and sweet group. The USDA recommends people to avoid this group as much as possible. Fats and oils are considered bad on the 1965 Food Pyramid.

A Guide to Daily Food Choices – USDA Guide 1960s

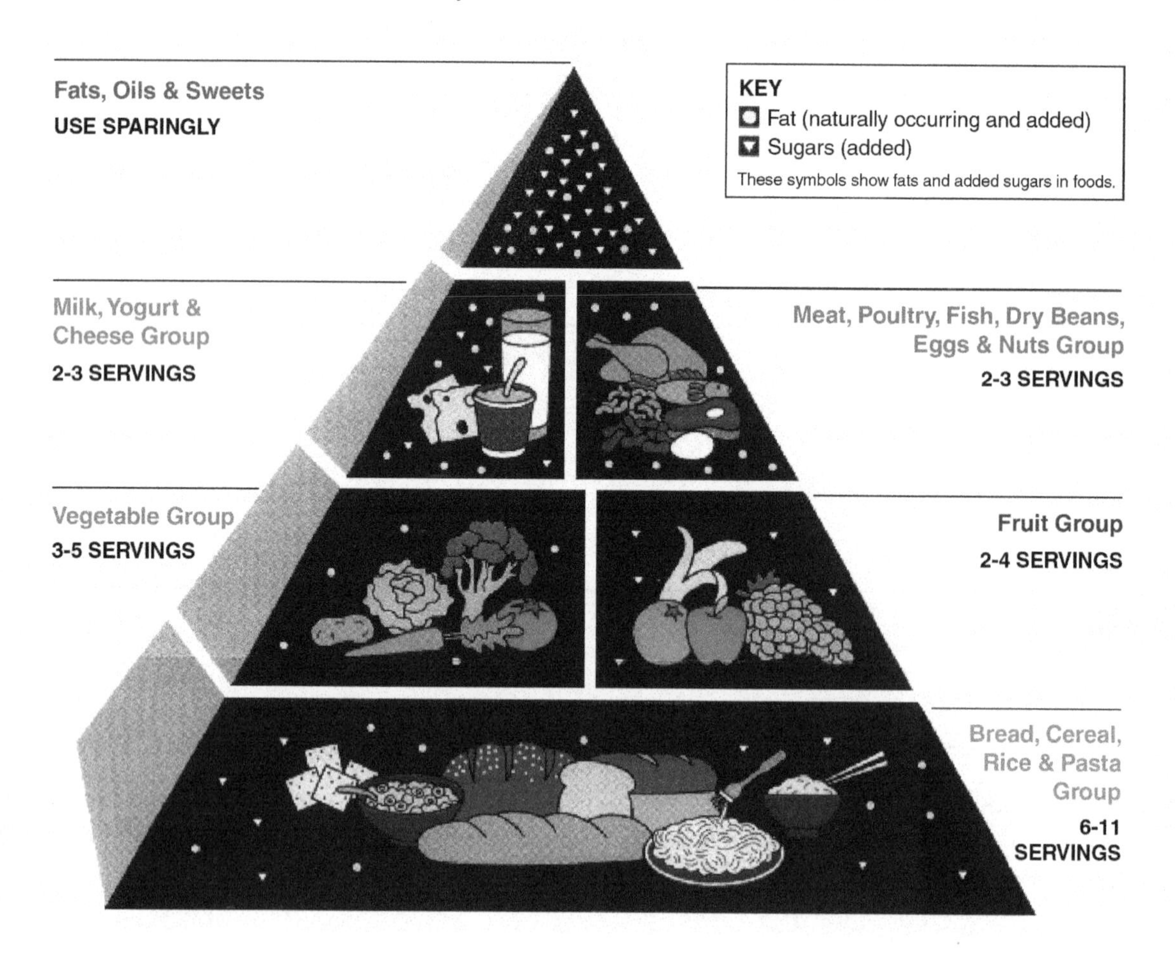

On the other hand, Robert is following the high-protein, low-carbohydrate diet made famous in the late 1990s in best-selling diet books such as *The South Beach Diet* and *The Atkins' Diet Revolution*. Dieters focus on proteins: they can eat as much meat as they want. Robert's huge hamburger is perfectly okay on this diet. However, people on low-carb diets seriously limit the amount of bread, pasta, rice, potatoes, and sweets. The word *carbohydrate* became a bad word in nutrition. In supermarkets all over America, shoppers could find low-carb bread, low-carb crackers, even low-carb pizzas. The largest part of the 1965 USDA Food Pyramid is the bread and grains group. The recommendation was eight to eleven portions a day. With the South Beach Diet and the Atkins' Plan, dieters were told to limit their carbohydrates to just two portions per day. For this reason, Robert is eating his big burger on a lettuce leaf, not a bun.

In 2005, the USDA issued a new food guide (MyPlate). It presents a much more balanced plan than either the 1965 version or the low-carb, high-protein diet. It is recommended that people eat as much fruit and vegetables as bread and grains. Meat portions are reduced, but the recommended milk intake has increased.

Basheera Designs/Shutterstock.com

Robert and Henry still have lunch every Thursday at the Tic Toc Diner on the highway. They are still a little overweight. They both order the Diet Special: grilled fish with green beans and carrots, with a small amount of rice, and a piece of bread. They are following the 2005 USDA Food Guide. When they finish eating, they are still not completely full or completely satisfied. "Oh well," says Robert, "I guess nothing's perfect. At least we can eat the bread and rice." "Maybe on the next diet we will be able to eat chocolate cake for dessert," says Henry. "Now that would be a great diet!"

True or False. Tell if the statement is true (T) or false (F). If it is false, correct it.

1. ___ People on low-carb diets should eat more bread and pasta than meat.
2. ___ The new USDA Food Pyramid recommends a more balanced diet than the 1965 version.
3 ___ Pasta companies are making more money now than ever before.
4. ___ The largest food group in the 1960s Food Pyramid is composed of bread, pasta, and rice.
5. ___ People on a low-carb diet can eat candy and chocolates, but no pasta.
6. ___ Dieters following the food pyramid limit the grams of fat they eat.
7. ___ Followers of the Atkins Diet think that carbohydrates are an important source of energy and vitamins.
8. ___ Dieters watching their carb count may eat bacon, ham, beef, bananas, and melons.
9. ___ According to the USDA Food Pyramid, people should eat two to four servings of fruit and three to five servings of vegetables per day.
10. ___ Bacon and eggs are an excellent breakfast according to the Food Pyramid.

Mark an X in the box for the plan where you can eat more of the following items.

PRODUCT	USDA FOOD PYRAMID	HIGH-PROTEIN, LOW-CARB DIET
bread	X	
fruit		
steak		
chicken		
butter		
rice		
vegetables		
cheese		
eggs		
bacon		
pasta		
bagels		
fish		

Match the term with its definition.

1. ___fad	a. used to
2. ___obsession	b. milk, eggs, and cheese
3. ___accustomed	c. chicken, turkey, and duck
4. ___poultry	d. keep it up
5. ___dissatisfied	e. slow but sure
6. ___dairy	f. the answer to a problem
7. ___restricted	g. a fixed idea in the mind, craziness
8. ___ solution	h. something that is very popular but just for a short time
9. ___ sustain	i. unhappy with something
10. ___ gradual	j. off limits

THE FOOD JOURNAL

Many dieticians say that people gain weight because they do not realize how much they really eat. One way to control the situation is to keep a food journal. For the next two weeks, you are going to write down everything you eat.

Before you go to sleep every night, make a quick list of all the things that you ate during the day. Do not forget to include snacks and other food that you eat that are not part of your regular meals. Also write down everything that you drink.

Be conscious of what you eat. On the bottom of the day's journal entry, there is space for comments. Write down your ideas about the quality of the food you ate, and what food group represents the highest percentage of your food. Analyze whether you think it was a good day or a bad day for eating.

Continue this activity for fourteen consecutive days.

mangostock/Shutterstock.com

WEEKLY FOOD JOURNAL

MONDAY	TUESDAY	WEDNESDAY	THURSDAY	FRIDAY	SATURDAY	SUNDAY
BREAKFAST	BREAKFAST	BREAKFAST	BREAKFAST	BREAKFAST	BREAKFAST	BREAKFAST
LUNCH	LUNCH	LUNCH	LUNCH	LUNCH	LUNCH	LUNCH
SNACK	SNACK	SNACK	SNACK	SNACK	SNACK	SNACK
DINNER	DINNER	DINNER	DINNER	DINNER	DINNER	DINNER

WEEKLY FOOD JOURNAL

MONDAY	TUESDAY	WEDNESDAY	THURSDAY	FRIDAY	SATURDAY	SUNDAY
BREAKFAST	BREAKFAST	BREAKFAST	BREAKFAST	BREAKFAST	BREAKFAST	BREAKFAST
LUNCH	LUNCH	LUNCH	LUNCH	LUNCH	LUNCH	LUNCH
SNACK	SNACK	SNACK	SNACK	SNACK	SNACK	SNACK
DINNER	DINNER	DINNER	DINNER	DINNER	DINNER	DINNER

FOOD SURVEY

At the end of the two-week period in which you kept a food journal, fill out this food survey.

1.	During these two weeks, I ate	a) normally	b) more than usual	c) less than usual
2.	My biggest meal of the day was	a) breakfast	b) lunch	c) dinner
3.	The average number of snacks per day	a) one	b) two-three	c) four or more
4.	In terms of carbohydrates, I ate	a) few	b) average	c) many
5.	My sugar intake was	a) low	b) average	c) high
6.	My meat intake was	a) low	b) average	c) high
7.	My dairy intake was	a) low	b) average	c) high
8.	My fruit intake was	a) low	b) average	c) high
9.	My vegetable intake was	a) low	b) average	c) high
10.	Did I pay more attention to food these two weeks?		a) yes	b) no
11.	What food did I eat the most often?	________________		

© Theo Solomon

12. How much junk food did I eat? a) a little b) a normal amount c) a lot

13. How many times did I eat out? a) none b) one-two c) three or more

14. Did I eat in the car these two weeks? a) yes b) no

15. If I ate in the car, what did I eat? a) breakfast b) lunch c) dinner d) snack

16. Did I eat after 8:00 p.m.? a) yes b) no

17. Did I eat breakfast every day? a) yes b) no

18. The overall quality of my food was a) high b) regular c) low

19. Was I satisfied with my diet over these two weeks? a) yes b) no

20. Will I continue to eat this way? a) yes b) no

Writing Assignment 9

Analysis of Eating Habits

Write a twelve-sentence paragraph based on your experience with the two-week analysis of your eating habits. Use your food journal and the survey to organize your ideas. Structure your paragraph in this way:

Sentence 1: Introduce the fact that you kept a food journal.

Sentences 2-9 Tell what you ate, what food group is the most attractive for you, and what meal was the largest.

Sentences 10-11: Discuss the snacks that you ate these two weeks.

Sentence 12: Indicate if you ate normally or changed your diet because you knew that you were keeping a food journal.

CHAPTER 6

Chronological Order

UNIT 1: NARRATION WRITING
UNIT 2: GIVING ADVICE AND DIRECTIONS: PROCESS PARAGRAPHS

UNIT 1: NARRATION WRITING

You use narration all the time. Some of the common uses of narration are:

- To tell about something that happened to you
- To discuss an incident that you remember from your past
- To explain to someone the plot of a movie, a television program, or a book
- To tell a story (a fable, a fairy tale, a myth)
- To tell a joke
- To describe important events (a hurricane, a war, an election)
- To tell what happened in a football, baseball, basketball, or soccer game
- To analyze an *action* or a *series of actions*—for this we use time order or chronological order

PARAGRAPH CHART FOR USING NARRATION: TELLING STORIES AND NARRATING EVENTS

Verb tenses used	1. The simple past tense a. regular verbs: add *-ed* b. consult a list of irregular past tense forms c. the past tense verb form is the same for all subjects 2. The past progressive (past continuous) a. *was* or *were* + the *-ing* form of the verb b. used for continuous action c. used with *while* and *at precisely* ...
Note on verbs	The sentence with *while* is a complex sentence (*While* SV, SV). *While I was jogging in the park, I saw my friend.* Note that the **progressive verb** goes with *while.*
Organization	Chronological order (time order)
Discourse markers	*First, second, third, next, after that, then, finally*; time clause words (*after, before, while, as soon as, once*)
Punctuation of discourse markers	- Place a comma after the discourse marker to introduce the sentence *First, you should try to speak at least an hour a day.* *After that, your English will improve.* - **Then** is not followed by a comma *Then you should try to walk three times a week.*
Topic sentence	The topic sentence for narration paragraphs introduces the "story." *The time I went to Rome was the most exciting in my life.* *My most embarrassing experience happened in May 2001.*
Concluding sentence	The conclusion could be the last action: *Finally, we paid the outrageous bill and made our way back to the hotel.* Or else, you could give a summary sentence: *I will never forget that day as long as I live.*
Grammar points	1. Since the paragraph is written in the past tense, make sure of the irregular verb forms. Check your grammar book. 2. You will probably write time clauses. When you begin with the time word and a subject and verb, place a comma before the next clause. *When I saw my mother, I started to cry.* *After I ran away from the robber, I stopped to rest.* *Before I went to bed, I checked all the locks.*
Grammar note	Keep a list of the irregular past tense verbs that you use (a verb journal) so that you learn as you write.

PARAGRAPH OF NARRATION

Verb tenses used: simple past
past progressive (*was* or *were* + *-ing* form of the verb)

Connectors (discourse markers)
Time words: *before*, *after*, *when*, *while*
Chronological order words: *first*, *then*, *after that*, *finally*

Order: Chronological order (time order)

Organization: Chronological outline

Activities yesterday

- woke up
- took a shower
- ate breakfast
- read the newspaper
- came to school
- went to work
- ate dinner
- wrote in my journal
- took time to study
- went to sleep

Yesterday was a busy day. I woke up at 6:00. Then I took a shower. After that, I ate breakfast. While I was eating breakfast, I read the newspaper. After that, I came to school. At school I took two courses. After school, I went to work. I worked six hours. When I came home from work, I had dinner. I ate chicken and rice. After dinner, I wrote in my journal. Before I went to sleep, I studied grammar for two hours.

Writing assignment: Write a chronological outline of your activities last Sunday. Then follow the outline to write a paragraph. Be sure to include time words and chronological order words in your writing.

Grammar in Context

THE IRREGULAR PAST TENSE

In paragraphs of narration, you often use the simple past tense. Many of the verbs in the simple past are irregular. Do the following activity to practice irregular past forms.

A. Write the irregular simple past form. Complete the chart.

Be	*was/were*	Become		Begin		Break	
Bring	*brought*	Build		Buy		Catch	
Choose		Come		Cost		Cut	
Dig		Do		Draw		Drink	
Drive		Eat		Fall		Feed	
Fight		Find		Fly		Forget	
Freeze		Get		Give		Go	
Grow		Have		Hear		Hide	
Hit		Hold		Hurt		Keep	
Know		Lead		Leave		Lend	
Let		Lose		Make		Mean	
Meet		Pay		Put		Quit	
Read		Ride		Ring		Rise	
Run		Say		See		Sell	
Send		Shake		Shoot		Shut	
Sing		Sleep		Speak		Spend	
Stand		Steal		Sweep		Swim	
Take		Teach		Tell		Think	
Throw		Wake		Win		Write	

B. Work with a partner to compose oral sentences using the past tense forms. Alternate: you do one sentence, your partner does the next, and so on.

C. Write down fifteen of your best sentences.

D. The class should write some of the sentences on the board and analyze the verb forms used.

E. Work with a different partner. Compose questions using the past tense. You ask a question and your partner gives a complete answer using the past tense. Switch roles for the next verb (your partner asks the question, and you give the answer). Remember the correct question form for the past tense (*Did* + subject [*you*, *he*, etc.] + *base form* + the rest of the sentence).

Did you eat pizza for dinner last night?
No, I didn't eat pizza. I ate chicken and rice.

Did John read a good story in the reading textbook?
Yes, he did. He read a story about a very interesting dog.

The Writing Workout Page

NARRATIONS

Now, of course, you are an adult. You are a "grownup." But when was the first time that you felt like an adult? Maybe it was your first dance or the first time you went camping with your friends. Maybe it was your first concert. When was the moment when you stopped thinking and feeling like a kid and started to feel grown up?	
You have probably taken vacations and day trips with your family and friends. Write a good travel story: exciting, funny, or terrible. Tell about something interesting that happened in your travels.	

Narrate what happened when you first found out that you were coming to America. Where were you? Who told you? What was your immediate reaction? Were you really happy or sad? Or did you have mixed feelings? How long did you have to prepare before you came to the United States?	
Many people are afraid of things. Some are afraid of heights. Others fear snakes or dogs. Still others are afraid of the dark. Tell a story about a time that you felt really afraid of something (or someone).	
It is time to tell a grandmother or a grandfather story. Write a narration in which you tell something that you did with one of your grandparents. It might be a special occasion or a typical Sunday afternoon.	

Writing Assignment 1

Making a Chronological Outline

Read the following tale adapted from Aesop, an Egyptian writer who lived as a slave in ancient Greece.

THE SAD TALE OF FROG AND SNAKE

Once upon a time there was a frog. The frog was a happy creature. She loved to jump from rock to rock and play around in the water. She especially loved the springtime when the water in the river was so high that it was exciting. One day, Frog was relaxing on the river bank. Snake slithered over to Frog and said, "Good morning, Frog. How are you today?"

"I am fine, Snake. What's going on?"

"I want to get to the other side of the river to visit my brother, but I can't swim. Can you give me a ride on your back?"

"I don't know," said Frog. "You know that snakes love to eat frogs."

"That's true," said Snake. "But I promise you that if you take me across, I'll be your best friend. I promise I will not bite you or eat you."

"Really? That is wonderful! I have always wanted a snake as a friend."

So Snake jumped up on Frog's back. Then Frog jumped from rock to rock. Snake was heavy, but Frog didn't mind. She was happy to help Snake. While she was moving across the river, Frog sang a song. Snake didn't say a word. He was a little afraid of the high water.

When they got to the other side of the river, Snake jumped off Frog's back.

"Well, here we are," said Frog. "So you will be my friend?" As soon as Frog asked this question, Snake took a big bite out of Frog's leg.

Next, he started to bite her feet and her neck. "What are you doing, Snake?" asked Frog terrified. "You promised that you would not bite me."

"I can't do anything about it," said Snake. "Do you know why?"

"No, I can't understand it," said Frog, in terrible pain.

"It's because I'm a Snake."

And so Snake ate Frog all up.

Writing Assignment 2

Retelling the Story: Making a Chronological Outline

A chronological outline traces the plot of the story in time order. Do not write complete sentences, just notes. The beginning of "The Sad Tale of Frog and Snake" has been done. Continue to the end.

1. Frog: happy creature
2. Played: river bank
3. Loved to jump on rocks
4. One day, Snake came
5.
6.
7.
8.
9.
10.

Retelling the story aloud
After you read the story about Frog and Snake and write the chronological outline, practice retelling the story aloud. Go around the class with each student recounting one incident. Then work in pairs and tell the story to each other.

Text-based writing assignment
Do you know a short fable from your culture, a story that your mother, father, aunt, grandmother, or grandfather used to tell you when you were a child? Write a fable that has a special meaning to you.

Grammar in Context

Exercise on "The Sad Tale of Frog and Snake"

Use a highlighter to mark all the time words in the story (*when*, *while*, etc.). Then circle the verbs. Study the past tense used in the narration portion (when the characters talk, they do so in the present or future).

Write the time words and the transition words from the story here:

________________________ ________________________

________________________ ________________________

________________________ ________________________

________________________ ________________________

Analyze the following complex sentences from the story.

Sentence 1: *While she was moving across the river, Frog sang a song.*

Time word: __________
Subject in the time clause: __________
Verb in the time clause: __________
Verb tense in the time clause: __________
Subject in the main clause: __________
Verb in the main clause: __________
Verb tense in the main clause: __________

Sentence 2: *When he got to the other side of the river, Snake jumped off Frog's back.*

Time word: __________
Subject in the time clause: __________
Verb in the time clause: __________
Verb tense in the time clause: __________
Subject in the main clause: __________
Verb in the main clause: __________
Verb tense in the main clause: __________

Sentence 3: *As soon as Frog asked this question, Snake took a bite out of Frog's leg.*

Time words: ____________
Subject in the time clause: ____________
Verb in the time clause: ____________
Verb tense in the time clause: ____________
Subject in the main clause: ____________
Verb in the main clause: ____________
Verb tense in the main clause: ____________

Sentence 4: *Next, he started to bite her feet and her neck.*

Time word: ____________
Punctuation in the sentence: ____________
Verb in the sentence: ____________
Verb tense in the sentence: ____________
Subject in the sentence: ____________

Writing Assignment 3

Making Chronological Outlines

Write fast chronological outlines for the following:

1. What did you do last summer? Write a quick outline of all your activities for the season. Remember that you do not have to write complete sentences (June: took grammar class; August: went on vacation).
   -
   -
   -
   -
   -
   -
   -
   -
2. Watch a television program, one that has a story. Write a chronological outline of the plot.
   -
   -
   -
   -
   -
   -
   -
   -
3. Write a chronological outline of your favorite movie.
   -
   -
   -
   -
   -
   -
   -
   -
4. Write a chronological outline of a story that you have read (*Tippy the War Hero*, *The Emperor's New Clothes*, etc.).
   -
   -
   -
   -
   -
   -
   -
   -

Writing Assignment 4

Description of the Illustration

© Brian J. Altano

Lights! Camera! Action!

You are a screenwriter and the director has asked you to write a short story to describe the illustration. Use the past tense and tell a good story. The movie title is *The Attack of the Aliens* **(or** *The True Story of the Battle of Ozinzch***, or a better title than these if you can think of one).**

Writing Assignment 5

Story Conclusions

The following passages are the beginning of two stories. Your task is to continue them and to write a conclusion. Make a chronological outline of your ideas. Then write eight to ten sentences to conclude the story. Remember to use the past tense.

Passage 1

I will never forget the day when I came to this college for the first time. It was a warm day in September. I drove from my house. While I was driving, I thought about my English classes. I wondered about my teachers. I parked my car and walked to the main classroom building. Then I walked through the doors and saw …

Passage 2

I saw a man with a large scar on his cheek. He came over to me and started talking to me. While we were talking, I didn't take my eyes off his scar. Finally, I couldn't take it anymore. I had to ask him.

I asked, "How did you get that scar on your face?"

He answered me, "It's a long story. I was fifteen years old at the time, and I was not always a calm boy. My friends were John, Nick, and Joe. These three were really wild. One day Nick said, "Let's do something wild and dangerous!" Let's …

Writing Assignment 6

A First for Everything

ON STAGE: PERFORMING AT A HIP-HOP CONCERT
By Dan Altano

© Isabella Altano

© Isabella Altano

© Isabella Altano

MY FIRST SHOW

I will never forget my first big concert. I finally got to sing with my rock band at a restaurant-bar near my University. I was really excited but also nervous. Singing has been my favorite activity since I was a little boy. When I went to college I started a band with my friends.

My family visited me from far away to see me perform so I was happy that they were there to watch. My girlfriend also came to see me sing. Before I left for the show I practiced my songs to make sure I remembered the words. After practicing, I drank tea with honey so my voice would sound better. The people in my band are a lot of fun to play music with and they are great musicians.

When I went on stage I saw all of my friends in the crowd and I was no longer nervous. I played my first song and everyone cheered! I sang for one hour and afterwards was very tired from jumping up and down. It was nice to hear that my friends enjoyed listening to my music. My first show was so much fun and it is a great memory.

Writing assignment: Write a paragraph in which you describe the first time that you did something: your first music lesson, your first soccer game, your first day in English class, your first speech, the first time you drove a car, or the first time that you cooked a meal.

Writing Assignment 7

Paragraph of Narration

HOW I FOUND OUT THAT ALL PEOPLE ARE NOT GOOD

When you are young, you probably believe that all people are sweet, nice, and good. They always want to help you. They are never jealous. They often think about other people's feelings more than their own. They are generous, kind, and never selfish. You are happy. But you are also naïve. Not everyone is like that. In fact, some people are just plain bad. They think only of themselves. They don't care about anyone but themselves.

Write a paragraph of narration. Tell the story of how you found out that some people are not very good. Write about a bad interpersonal relationship. Write the paragraph on a separate sheet of paper to hand in for correction and a grade.

- Write a chronological outline.
- Follow the outline to write your paragraph.
- Make sure that the past tense verb forms that you use are correct.

Outline:

-
-
-
-
-
-
-
-
-
-
-

Writing Assignment 8

Paragraph of Narration

HOW I MET MY BEST FRIEND

It seems as if you have always known each other. You know each other's deepest secrets. You are inseparable. But how did you meet? Write a paragraph of narration in which you tell the story of how you met your best friend or your boyfriend, girlfriend, wife, husband, or partner. Write a quick outline and follow it in your writing.

Outline:

-

-

-

-

-

-

-

-

-

-

-

-

Writing Assignment 9

Journal Practice: The Dream Journal

In 1900, Sigmund Freud, an Austrian psychiatrist and the father of psychoanalysis, wrote *The Interpretation of Dreams*. In this book, he said that in our dreams we reveal our true selves. Our dreams tell our real feelings, likes, dislikes, fears, and desires. Some people like to talk about their dreams and discuss their deep meaning.

For the next two weeks, you will keep a dream journal. Try to pay particular attention to your dreams. Keep a notebook and a pen next to your bed. As soon as you wake up in the morning, write a quick chronological outline about your dream. Then sometime later in the day, write a narration paragraph telling the story of your dream. Do this for two weeks. If you don't dream or you don't remember your dream, write a paragraph about other dreams that you have had in your life. If you don't remember any dreams, then describe a daydream.

DREAM JOURNAL – WEEK 1

Dream – Day 1	Dream – Day 2	Dream – Day 3
Notes on your dream:	Notes on your dream	Notes on your dream

Dream – Day 4	Dream – Day 5	Dream – Day 6	Dream – Day 7
Notes on your dream	Notes on your dream	Notes on your dream	Notes on your dream

DREAM JOURNAL – WEEK 2

Dream – Day 1	Dream – Day 2	Dream – Day 3
Notes on your dream:	Notes on your dream	Notes on your dream

Dream – Day 4	Dream – Day 5	Dream – Day 6	Dream – Day 7
Notes on your dream	Notes on your dream	Notes on your dream	Notes on your dream

Dream questionnaire

At the end of your two-week experience recording your dreams, answer the following questions.

1. How many times did you dream in two weeks? 1–2 3–4 5–6 Every day

2. Did you remember most of your dreams? _______

3. Categories of dreams: (how many of each type)
   a. Nightmare __________
   b. Fantasy __________
   c. Someone chasing you (you are running away) __________
   d. Dreams of someone no longer alive __________
   e. Another type: ____________ how many: __________
   f. Another type: ____________ how many: __________

4. Do you feel that dreams have deep meaning? __________ What meaning do your dreams have?

5. If you want help in interpreting your dreams, whom do you talk to? ______________

6. Do you believe that dreams tell us something about the future? _______ Explain.

Journal-based writing: Write in ten to twelve sentences about your dreams during the journal period. Tell how many times you dreamed, what type of dreams you had, and if these dreams had any deep meaning for you. If you did not dream, or if you do not recall your dreams, write about the general subject of dreams in your life. Tell if you usually dream. Also indicate some of the most powerful dreams in your life. Finally, if you never dream, interview a few people and write about their dreams.

UNIT 2: GIVING ADVICE AND DIRECTIONS: PROCESS PARAGRAPHS

People love to give advice. It makes them feel useful and important. They like telling others what to do and how to do something. This is particularly true with problems. Some people are "problem solvers": they are good listeners, and give advice about how to make the problem disappear.

Many people enjoy giving advice on love and family relationships, saving money, and learning a new skill. They also give directions: how to drive to their house or how to get to a restaurant or club, the movies, or a beautiful spot in nature.

Bookstores are filled with "how-to" texts such as:

- *Cookbooks* that present recipes and tell how to prepare dishes
- *Weight loss* books that explain the latest diet to help people lose weight and make them thinner
- *Computer manuals* that explain how to run a particular program
- *Guidebooks* or *travel books* that tell what to see, where to eat, and what to do when visiting a special place

PARAGRAPH CHART FOR GIVING ADVICE AND DIRECTIONS: PROCESS PARAGRAPHS

Verb forms used	1. Modals of advisability: a. *should* b. *have to* c. *must* 2. Modals of possibility: a. *might* b. *may* c. *could* 3. Imperatives (commands) - Use the base form of the verb - Do not use YOU or any other subject in the sentence
Note on verbs	You should alternate between modals and imperatives throughout the paragraph.
Organization	By steps or phases
Discourse markers	*First, second, third* (etc.), *next, after that, then, in addition*
Punctuation of discourse markers	- Place a comma after the discourse marker *First, you should try to speak at least an hour a day.* *After that, your English will improve.* - **Then** is not followed by a comma *Then you should try to walk three times a week.* - **In addition** begins a sentence. Place a comma after it.
Topic sentence	If you want to … , follow my advice. *If you want to be happy, follow my advice.* *If you would like to learn Korean, follow my directions.*
Concluding sentence	Reverse the topic sentence. Put the second clause first and the first clause second. Use the future tense in the second clause. *If you follow my advice, you will learn to cook pasta.* *If you follow my directions, you will speak very clearly.*
Grammar points	1. Between the two clauses in the topic sentence and the conclusion, place a comma. 2. Pay attention to modals. ***Should, must, might, may***, and ***could*** are followed by the *base form*. ***Have*** and ***have got*** are followed by the *infinitive*. 3. You form the imperative with the *base form* of the verb. Imperatives do not change according to singular or plural or different levels of respect. You use the same form when you are speaking to your dog, your friend, your boss, or ten people.
Grammar note	The word ***advice*** is non-count and always singular. Use the adjective *some* before it. (Please give me *some advice*.)

Writing Assignment 1

Making Bullet Lists

TIPS FOR INCREASING YOUR VOCABULARY

Steps:

- Always keep a dictionary handy.
- Highlight or underline new words in everything you read.
- Pay close attention to the context of the word.
- Keep a separate vocabulary notebook.
- Divide the vocabulary notebook into categories (cooking, sports, art, school, grammar).
- When you write down a new word, try to figure out if it has a prefix, a suffix, or a stem that helps you learn the meaning.
- Review your vocabulary notebook often.
- If the word is hard to pronounce, make notes on the correct pronunciation.

Paragraph:

One challenging aspect of studying a language is learning new vocabulary words. Having a good vocabulary is very important. You need it to understand what you read and to make it easier to explain yourself when you write or speak to others. Here are a few tips to help you increase your vocabulary. First of all, always keep a dictionary handy. You never know when you are going to need it. Pocket dictionaries and electronic dictionaries are excellent because they are portable. Next, always use a highlighter when you read, to mark a new word. When you read a sentence, pay particular attention to the context. Is the word positive or negative? You can tell if you pay attention to context. Is it a noun or verb? If it is an adjective, what noun does it describe? When you find a new word, you should write it down in a separate vocabulary notebook. Divide the notebook into sections on different subjects and make a special section for words related to what you want to study. You might write down prefixes, suffixes, or stems that can help you learn the meaning. You should review your vocabulary notebook often. Make the new words become like old friends. Remember to indicate the correct pronunciation for difficult words. If you follow my instructions, you will have a strong vocabulary very soon.

A. Underline all the imperatives in the paragraph.

B. Circle all the modals used.

C. Highlight the conclusion.

D. Number the steps in developing a strong vocabulary.

Writing Assignment 2

Making Bullet Lists

Study the bullet list after the title ***Tips for Increasing Your Vocabulary.*** The writer indicates eight steps to be followed to increase vocabulary. Now reread the paragraph. Did you notice how the writer followed the outline in order? The writer adds a little supporting information and a few examples, but the bullets are followed precisely. This is an excellent way to organize process paragraphs. In this exercise, you will practice making bulleted lists.

1. **How to clean the house in 30 minutes when you just remember that a friend is visiting**
   - Start in kitchen: dishes, countertop, floor
   - Next,
   -
   -
   -
   -

2. **How to make the perfect cup of tea or coffee**
   - Make sure to use bottled water.
   -
   -
   -
   -
   -

3. **How to look really nice for a big date**
   - Take a long shower. Wash everywhere, even behind your ears and inside your nose.
   -
   -
   -
   -
   -

4. **How to talk someone into doing something that you want to do but he or she doesn't really feel like doing**
   -
   -
   -
   -
   -

Homework assignment: Make bulleted lists for the following topics:

1. How to keep your bedroom clean all the time
2. How to cook a nice breakfast
3. How to dance
4. How to meet interesting people

Writing Assignment 3

Editing Checklist

After you finish writing, but before you hand in your paragraph to the professor for a grade, you should follow the steps on the Editing Checklist. This will ensure that you avoid simple mistakes. If you follow this process, you will probably correct some errors and receive a higher grade. After you complete the step, place on check on the line.

___ Underline all the verbs.

___ Check that the verbs agree with the subject (S/V agreement).

___ Make sure that the verb tense is correct. Remember to be consistent.

___ **Circle** all the commas.

___ Should they be commas, or perhaps periods? Make sure you don't have run-on sentences.

___ **Put a box** around all the adjectives.

___ Have you used the correct form of the word? Remember that *-ed* is often used for people and the *-ing* ending is generally used for things (i.e., a bor**ing** movie makes you bor**ed**; you feel interest**ed** in an interest**ing** topic).

___ Check all words for spelling. If you have made a mistake, correct it. Then write the word in a special spelling journal that you use for misspelled words.

___ Make sure that the topic sentence and the concluding sentence are excellent. Remember that these make important first and last impressions.

Grammar in Context

IMPERATIVES AND MODALS

When you write process paragraphs, the verb forms that you use are *imperatives* and *modals*. Let us examine these forms.

Imperatives

To form the imperative, use the *base form* of the verb (the dictionary form). There is no tense. Also, there is no singular or plural form, and no difference between polite and familiar, as there is in some languages. The word *please* is used at the beginning or the end of the sentence. **Do not use** the word *you* in the imperative sentence. No subject is used at all. Thus, the sentence begins with *Please* or with the *imperative verb*. The negative command is *Don't* + base form.

Please check the oil.
Eat your broccoli, Billy.
Hand in your papers, please.
Tell him to leave.
Don't talk to me like that. I'm your older brother.

Modals

Modals are used for ability, possibility, permission, advice, and necessity. Almost all modals are followed by the base form of the verb. Only ***have*** and ***have got*** (necessity) are followed by an infinitive [I have *to go*]. Study the sample sentences below.

Ability (*can*)

I *can* speak three languages.
Can you play the piano or the guitar?

Permission and requests (*may*, *could*, *would*, *can*)

May I speak with you? [more formal]
Could I borrow your dictionary?
Would you pass the salt, please.
Can you give me a ride home? [less formal]

Possibility (*may*, *might*, *could*)

My brother *may* cook turkey tonight for dinner.
He *might* make hamburgers and French fries.
He *could* just buy a pizza. [a little less possible]

Necessity

Beatriz *must* study because her final exam in math is tomorrow.
Nestor *has* **to leave** early tomorrow morning for work.
I *have got* **to clean** my room. It's so messy that I can't find my shoes.

Advice

You *should* take Professor Lynch's class. She's the best.
Tess *should* learn to drive, so she doesn't have to take two buses to get to school.

Exercise 1: Error Correction

Underline the mistakes in each sentence. Then write the sentence correctly.

1. You getting too thin. You don't stay on a diet no more.

   ____.

2. Take Main Street and you make a right at Crescent Avenue.

   ____.

3. You should to see the new Harry Potter movie. Its' fantastic.

   ____.

4. Would you borrow me your dictionary for one minutes.

   ____.

5. You sit down. I bring you a cup coffee in a moments.

   ____.

6. I have leave now. I don't want be late for class.

   ____.

7. Can I speaking with you after the class end?

   ____.

8. You should studied harder, and you gets better grades.

   ____.

9. Go to the cafeteria and you wait for me. I be there in five minutes.

   ____.

10. You put please $10 of gas in the my car.

    ____.

11. Tomorrow I have three possibilities. I may to stay home. I could have go to the beach. I might going to the movie.

    ____.

    ____.

12. May you give me a ride home after class. I must to get there immediately.

    ____.

Exercise 2: Sentence Stems

Write conclusions to the sentences. Use modals or imperatives.

1. To get an A in writing class, ______________________.
2. I'm not sure whom I will call first. I __________ my mother, or I _______ my boss.
3. You are gaining a little weight. You ______________________.
4. Don't worry. ______________________.
5. You wrote a terrible paragraph. The next time ______________________.
6. When you see my ex-girlfriend, ______________________.
7. It's already one o'clock in the morning. We ______________________.
8. Henry is sixteen. When he comes home late, his father says ______________________.
9. Jesse is very talented. He ______________ the guitar and sing, too.
10. It's very cold outside. ______________________.

Exercise 3: Sentence Conclusions

Write a beginning for each sentence.

1. ______________________________ when he saw her wedding ring.
2. ______________________________ and don't ever call me again either.
3. ______________________________ a doctor about your bad leg.
4. ______________________________ or I might just stay home and watch TV.
5. ______________________________ where the library is?
6. ______________________________ Spanish, English, and a little German.
7. ______________________________ fall asleep when you are driving.
8. ______________________________ leave before my mother gets home.
9. ______________________________ borrow $5.00 until tomorrow?
10. ______________________________ harder if you want to make more money.

The Writing Workout Page

MODERN MANNERS

Since many consider you a person who understands manners, they often ask you for advice. Provide an answer to the following questions on manners, or rules of behavior.

I have a job at an office. I sit right across from a woman who often leaves her cellphone on her desk when she goes out to lunch or for a break. Her phone rings all the time. The ring is a really annoying train whistle. Is it good manners to answer her personal cellphone or turn it off?

I love soccer and often go to watch my little sister play. She is 10 years old. The game is very exciting. My problem is that many of the parents and relatives of the girls stand right on the sideline and shout all the time. They yell at the referee, the other players, and even at the other parents. How can I explain to them that they are behaving in a very rude manner?

I ride the bus to school. I consider myself a very polite person. Yesterday, I was sitting on the bus reading my textbook. The bus was very crowded. In front of me there were two people standing up. One of them was a pregnant woman. The other one was a very elderly man. I stood up to give up my seat. But then I didn't know who to give it to. Who deserves the seat more, a pregnant woman or a senior citizen?

I have a lively email correspondence with my friends. Some live in my native country, and others live in various parts of the United States. Many of them get mad at me and call me lazy and a bad friend because I usually take four or five days to answer an email. Is there a particular deadline for answering email messages?

I like to go out to lunch with my friends. However, one of my friends has an annoying habit. As soon as we sit down to eat and order, she calls her boyfriend and talks with him for five minutes. I think that she is rude. Is it bad manners to talk on the cellphone when you are sitting with another person?

Homework: Write two "manner problems" on separate sheets of paper. Bring them to class. Exchange them with classmates. Your classmates will write answers to your situations, and you will write responses to theirs.

Writing Assignment 4

Letter Writing

HOW TO BE HAPPY

Life is difficult. People have many things to worry about: money, work, school, family, and friends. When they feel pressure and stress, many people get depressed. Maybe it is easier to give in to the negative feelings and to be unhappy. Open the newspaper, and you will read about murders, muggings, suicide bombers, and terrorist activities. Turn on the radio, and it is the same story. Listen to people talking, and they are discussing the latest news of conflicts overseas. Even nature sometimes makes people afraid: somewhere in the world there might be a hurricane, a tsunami, or an earthquake. In fact, in general, people are not very happy.

Suppose that you receive a long email from a good friend. Your friend lives in another city, many hours away from you. She describes her life. She is going to school and taking fifteeen credits of English language courses. In addition, she has a job at the mall. She works in a video game store. It is very loud in the store because they have four monitors where customers try out new games. Her co-workers are not very friendly. She lives at home with her mother and two sisters. She is very busy with school and work, so she doesn't have a lot a time to see her friends much. She doesn't have a partner. She is starting to get depressed and unhappy with her life.

Write a ten- to twelve-sentence letter to your friend in which you give her advice on how to be happy. Tell her what she should do to feel better about her life.

Writing Assignment 5

Description of the Photograph

OPTIMIST OR PESSIMIST

Present a description of the photograph. Do you believe that the storm is coming and that the ship is in danger? Or do you feel that the storm has already passed and that the danger is over?

Personally, how do you deal with events that make you afraid? How do you prepare for them? Give a few examples.

Mikadun/Shutterstock.com

Writing Assignment 6

The Friend Who Won't Leave

It's easy to be lonely living in a different country. You don't have many relatives here and you begin with very few friends. A welcome change is a visit from relatives or friends from your native country. Most of the time, these visits are short: a week or two. Sometimes, though, the visit extends beyond that term, and you are put into an uncomfortable situation.

Read the following situation.

You had a close friend in high school but you have not seen her for four or five years. Suddenly, she calls you up and tells you that she is coming to America. She wants to stay with you. You have nice memories of your friend even though you don't know what she's been doing for the last few years. She comes to your apartment and you are very happy to see her. She sleeps on the couch in your living room.

Your apartment is very small. With all her clothes and shoes in the living room, it always looks messy. In addition, you are very busy. You go to school and also have a job at a store in the mall. Your friend, whose name is Rose, stays in your apartment, listens to your stereo, watches your television, drinks your coffee, and eats your food. She doesn't offer to pay for much. However, she does say thank you all the time. She says that you really understand how to treat a guest. You enjoy her company, but at the same time, the apartment feels crowded.

There is one big problem: she will not leave. She didn't tell you how long she was going to stay in your apartment. You thought that it was going to be for a regular visit – one or two weeks. However, now a month has passed and she is still here. She shows no signs of leaving. She says that she loves staying with you, walking in the park two blocks away, and meeting new people.

You are becoming worried. Will she ever leave? You have been a good host, but now enough is enough. What can you do? What should you tell her? How should you talk about the subject?

Write a paragraph telling what you will do in this situation. You are a nice person and don't want to hurt your friend, but you are also worried that she wants to stay for months and months. Explain what you will tell her and how you will handle the situation. (To begin, make a bullet outline. Then write ten to twelve sentences.)

Writing Assignment 7

Think, Write, Pair, Share

Read the following situations. Think of advice that you can give. Write your ideas down in a few sentences in your notebook. Then work with a partner to discuss the matter. Share your ideas and listen to your partner's thoughts. Finally, be ready to talk about the situation with the whole class.

1. You have a close friend and classmate, James, who has been going out with a girl, Alice, for about six months. James really likes Alice, and it seems that they are very close. However, one Sunday afternoon you decide to take a walk in a park that has a beautiful mountain path. You are strolling along, enjoying nature and the nice day. As you turn a corner, you look down to a bench on the path below. Who is sitting on the bench? Alice, with another man. They are sitting very close, looking in each others' eyes, and holding hands. You continue to walk up the path. On your return a half hour later, they are still there, looking very happy together. This time you notice that you also know the man, an acquaintance of yours and James from school. His name is Joseph. You take a different path down so they won't see you. That evening your friend James calls to ask you to drive him to school the next day because he is having problems with his car. You don't know what to say. Should you tell him? Now? Or tomorrow morning in the car? Or should you just let it go and let him find out by himself?

2. You take the bus to work and walk seven blocks to the place where you work. Every day you pass five or six homeless people on the way. They are often the same ones. Many times they look hungry and cold. Their clothes are ragged. Most days, they ask you for money. Sometimes you give one of them a dollar. Then another one comes over and asks for a dollar, too. You want to be nice and generous, but to give each person a dollar every day means six dollars. That is what you spend on lunch. You are certainly not rich and work very hard for your money. What should you do in this situation?

3. You are a very serious student, and you usually study very hard. You feel that it is important to learn as much as possible in school, When it comes to tests, you study extra. You are always very prepared. Most of the time, you get either an A or a B. This is very satisfying to you. It is a reward for your hard work. However, there are a few other students in the class with a different attitude. They don't study much, and they are not prepared. During tests they cheat. One guy brings in a sheet with notes. He hides this page under his test paper and copies the answers. One woman always sits next to a really good student and copies her answers to the test. Another person has programmed his answers in his electronic dictionary. It's not just a dictionary, but really a mini-computer. You can type in other information such as the answers to test questions. These three "cheaters" are getting very good grades, sometimes even better grades than you get. This bothers you. What should you do? Should you confront them? Tell the professor? Talk about it with other non-cheaters in the class?

Writing Assignment 8

Letter of Advice

FINDING AN APARTMENT IN AMERICA

Suppose that you receive a letter from a good friend of yours from your country. She tells you that she is moving to America. She would like to know how to find a nice apartment. Write a letter back to her, giving her advice based on your personal experience and the experiences of other people that you know.

Verb forms: Imperatives and/or modals (*should*, etc.)
Organization: Steps (*first*, *second*, *then*, *after that*, etc.)
Vocabulary:

Real estate agent
Newspaper ad
Apartment
House
Condominium
Townhouse
First floor (second floor, etc.) [On the first floor: She lives on the first floor.]
Rent
To rent an apartment
Deposit (security deposit)
Lease (a long-term agreement to rent an apartment): a one-year lease
Neighbor
Neighborhood
Tenant (renter)
Landlord (owner)
Utilities (electricity, heat, water) [The *utilities* are included in the rent (you don't pay extra); or: The rent is $700. *Utilities* are extra.]
Location (where the apartment is). The apartment has an excellent location.

Give advice to your friend. Write on a separate piece of paper.

Dear ________________________,

Sincerely yours,

Writing Assignment 9

How to Celebrate a Favorite Holiday

HOLIDAYS

Americans celebrate several holidays throughout the year. On the Fourth of July, they celebrate the independence of the country from England. On Thanksgiving, they give thanks for all the good things that they have received during the year. On Christmas, Christians celebrate the birth of Christ by exchanging gifts. On Valentine's Day, lovers exchange flowers and romantic gifts. On Halloween, children dress up and go trick-or-treating. Many adults also wear costumes and go to costume parties.

1. First make an outline listing the ways that you celebrate your favorite holiday in your country.
2. Working in pairs, tell your partner about your holiday.
3. Listen closely as your partner tells about his or her favorite holiday.
4. Write a ten- to twelve-sentence process paragraph telling how people in your country celebrate the holiday you like the most.

Grammar Point

Make sure to use the plural noun to identify people from your country. For example:

Koreans usually make a special soup.
Colombians invite all their relatives to their house.
Polish people begin the holiday by going to church.
The **French** drink a special sweet wine after dinner.
The **Chinese** make noodles in many different ways.

© Isabella Altano

Writing Assignment 10

The Thank-you Letter

Writing a thank-you letter was a very common activity in the past. There were many occasions when people wrote notes of thanks: to thank people for their help, to express gratitude for a special gift received or special efforts made. In America, many people write short thank-you letters (and include gifts, often cash) in the holiday season at the end of the year. They say thank you to the letter carrier, the sanitation engineers (who collect the trash), elementary school teachers, co-workers, bosses, secretaries, and assistants at work.

Suppose that you were invited to a neighbor's house for dinner. They were Americans, who had lived in the area for many years. It was a wonderful evening. The food was excellent, and better yet, the hosts welcomed you very warmly into their house. They really showed you a great deal about American customs. The conversation was excellent, too. The hosts were very curious to learn about your culture and customs. It was a perfect evening.

Write a thank-you letter to your neighbors. Show gratitude for the food and their hospitality. Perhaps even invite them to your house for dinner.

The tone of this letter will probably be somewhat formal. This is the kind of letter that your neighbors will probably keep and maybe even show to other people because they will be so proud to have received it.

Writing Assignment 11

Giving Advice on How to Lose Weight

Many people are overweight. They do not get enough exercise. Probably they eat too much junk food. Also, most people eat too many snacks. In the evening, they sit on the couch and watch television. They eat a snack at 10:30 p.m. and then go to sleep. They eat donuts and bagels, cookies, and potato chips. It is not easy to stay the same weight, and very difficult to lose weight.

In a clearly written paragraph, give advice on how to lose weight.

Vocabulary

Work out (a verb) to get exercise	Mary *works out* at the gym.
Snack (noun) food eaten between meals	I eat cookies and cake for *snacks.*
Jog (verb) to run slowly and steadily	Nancy *jogs* two miles every morning.
Exercise (verb) to work out	You must *exercise* three times a week.
Exercise (noun) physical activity	Harold has to get more *exercise.*
Gym (noun) the place where you work out	Jim belongs to a *gym.*
Couch potato (noun) a person who just sits on the couch and doesn't exercise	My brother is a couch potato.
Diet (noun) when you eat less	Roger has to go on a *diet.* He is too fat.
Meal (noun) three organized times you eat every day	You should only eat three *meals* a day.
Breakfast, lunch, dinner	the three *meals*

Adjectives

Positive: *healthy*, *nutritious*, *delicious* [all three are used to describe food]
Negative: *fatty* and *oily* [full of oil], *greasy*, *fattening* [it makes you fat]

Topic Sentence: If you want to lose weight, follow my advice.

Giving Advice on Saving Money

HOW TO SAVE MONEY

Saving money is a very difficult, yet important thing. Suppose that your friend wants to save for something special, perhaps an anniversary or birthday gift, a special occasion, or even a house. Give advice on how to save as much money as possible.

First, write a bullet outline with details on the process. Then follow the outline to write the paragraph.

Writing Assignment 13

The English Conversation Journal

For the next two weeks, you will keep an English Conversation Journal. Record all the conversations that you have in English. Write down who you spoke with and what you talked about. Count the total number of conversations and the total minutes or hours that you spoke English during a day. Then rate yourself. How comfortable did you feel during these conversations? How effective were you in communicating? Rate yourself on a scale of 1 to 5 (1 is very comfortable / very effective and 5 is not comfortable at all / not effective at all; 3 is average). In the second week, make a strong effort to increase the time you speak in English. In the chart provided, record only the conversations that you had in English.

WEEK 1

Monday	**Tuesday**	**Wednesday**	**Thursday**
No. of conversations: __	No. of conversations: __	No. of conversations: __	No. of conversations: __
Who you spoke with:	Who you spoke with:	Who you spoke with:	Who you spoke with:
1.	1.	1.	1.
2.	2.	2.	2.
3.	3.	3.	3.
4.	4.	4.	4.
5.	5.	5.	5.
What you talked about:	What you talked about:	What you talked about:	What you talked about:
Total minutes / hours	Total minutes / hours	Total minutes / hours	Total minutes / hours
How comfortable were you? (scale of 1-5) ___	How comfortable were you? (scale of 1-5) ___	How comfortable were you? (scale of 1-5) ___	How comfortable were you? (scale of 1-5) ___
How effective were you? (scale of 1-5) ___	How effective were you? (scale of 1-5) ___	How effective were you? (scale of 1-5) ___	How effective were you? (scale of 1-5) ___

Friday	Saturday	Sunday	Weekly Summary
No. of conversations: __	No. of conversations: __	No. of conversations: __	No. of conversations for the whole week: _____
Who you spoke with:	Who you spoke with:	Who you spoke with:	
1.	1.	1.	
2.	2.	2.	Who were your best conversations with?
3.	3.	3.	1.
4.	4.	4.	2.
5.	5.	5.	3.
What you talked about:	What you talked about:	What you talked about:	4.
			Your favorite topics:
Total minutes / hours	Total minutes / hours	Total minutes / hours	Total minutes / hours for the week: _________
How comfortable were you? (scale of 1-5) ___	How comfortable were you? (scale of 1-5) ___	How comfortable were you? (scale of 1-5) ___	Level of satisfaction with your week's English speaking (scale of 1-5) _______
How effective were you? (scale of 1-5) ___	How effective were you? (scale of 1-5) ___	How effective were you? (scale of 1-5) ___	

WEEK 2

Monday	Tuesday	Wednesday	Thursday
No. of conversations: __	No. of conversations: __	No. of conversations: __	No. of conversations: __
Who you spoke with:	Who you spoke with:	Who you spoke with:	Who you spoke with:
1.	1.	1.	1.
2.	2.	2.	2.
3.	3.	3.	3.
4.	4.	4.	4.
5.	5.	5.	5.
What you talked about:	What you talked about:	What you talked about:	What you talked about:
Total minutes / hours	Total minutes / hours	Total minutes / hours	Total minutes / hours
How comfortable were you? (scale of 1-5) ___	How comfortable were you? (scale of 1-5) ___	How comfortable were you? (scale of 1-5) ___	How comfortable were you? (scale of 1-5) ___
How effective were you? (scale of 1-5) ___	How effective were you? (scale of 1-5) ___	How effective were you? (scale of 1-5) ___	How effective were you? (scale of 1-5) ___

Friday	Saturday	Sunday	Weekly Summary
No. of conversations: __	No. of conversations: __	No. of conversations: __	No. of conversations for the whole week: _____
Who you spoke with:	Who you spoke with:	Who you spoke with:	
1.	1.	1.	
2.	2.	2.	Who were your best conversations with?
3.	3.	3.	1.
4.	4.	4.	2.
5.	5.	5.	3.
What you talked about:	What you talked about:	What you talked about:	4.
			Your favorite topics:
Total minutes / hours	Total minutes / hours	Total minutes / hours	Total minutes / hours for the week: _________
How comfortable were you? (scale of 1-5) ___	How comfortable were you? (scale of 1-5) ___		Level of satisfaction with your week's English speaking (scale of 1-5) _______
How effective were you? (scale of 1-5) ___	How effective were you? (scale of 1-5) ___	How comfortable were you? (scale of 1-5) ___	
		How effective were you? (scale of 1-5) ___	

Journal-based writing assignment: Write a paragraph in which you summarize your journal activities for the two weeks. Explain how many conversations you had, who you spoke with, under what circumstances (at work, in class, on the bus, at home, with friends). Also indicate how you would rate yourself in terms of comfort and effectiveness.

CHAPTER 7

Ascending and Descending Order

OPINION WRITING

OPINION WRITING

Stating an opinion clearly and effectively is the sign of a well-developed mind. It is both an academic skill and a real-life skill. *Opinionated* people are constantly talking about how they feel about issues. They also tell what they think about movies, restaurants, stores, and other people. People have opinions about current issues: the performance of the president, the economy, the war, and guns in society. In speaking and in writing about opinions, it is important to organize your thoughts to present a strong opinion.

There are three **objects** or **purposes** in the opinion paragraph:

1. To state your opinion clearly and forcefully
2. To support your idea with strong proof
3. To persuade your readers to change their opinion to agree with you

Opinion writing is used in all academic courses. Opinions are often the topic of examination questions:
History: Do you feel that Abraham Lincoln was an effective president?
Psychology: Is nature or nurture more important in personality development?
Sociology: In your opinion, why are there so many murders each year in the United States?
Literature: Do you think that the plot of *Huckleberry Finn* is well organized?
Biology: Why do women live almost four years longer than men on the average?

PARAGRAPH CHART FOR THE OPINION PARAGRAPH

Verb forms used	Usually simple present; simple past for specific examples.
Key words	*I think that ...* *I feel that ...* *I believe that ...* *It is my opinion that ...*
Organization	Enumeration structure: according to the listing of reasons or proof to support your opinion.
Discourse markers	**Adding information words**: *furthermore, in addition, moreover* **Enumeration structure words**: *first, second, third, first of all, also, finally* **Reasons**: *One reason is; Another reason is; The third reason is ...*
Ascending and descending order	Where should you place the most important reason, first or last? Some writers prefer to begin with the strongest reason. They feel that it makes an immediate impact, a strong first impression. Others think that writers should build up from the weakest to the strongest opinion in order to leave a solid last impression. Both structures are valid. Try each of them to see which one you like more.
Topic sentence	The topic sentence for an opinion paragraph states: a. the issue b. your particular idea about the issue *I believe that capital punishment is wrong for the following reasons.* *There are several reasons why I think that Americans should study a foreign language.* *I feel that eating too much fast food is bad for your health.*
Concluding sentence	In the conclusion sentence, you should restate your topic sentence: *These are the reasons why I think that capital punishment is wrong.*
Grammar points	***Agreement and Disagreement*** Sometimes you are asked to agree or disagree with a statement. Here is the correct grammatical formation: *I agree with Ms. Johnson.* *I disagree with that opinion.* *I agree that they should not teach religion in public schools.* *I do not agree with you.* **Do not write**: I am agree with ...

The hero sandwich model: Opinion paragraphs

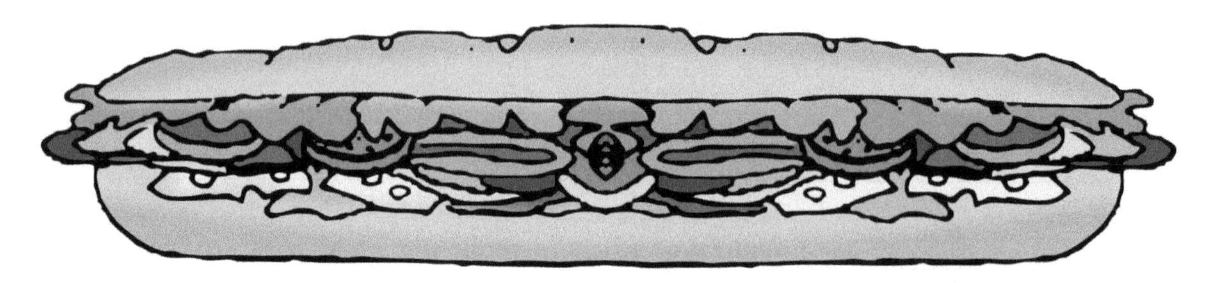

© Brian J. Altano

Let's make the structure of an opinion paragraph visual. Picture a hero sandwich (a sub). It has half a roll on the top, and half on the bottom. There is a layer of meat. On top of the meat is cheese. Above the cheese is lettuce and tomato. Thus, you could say that a good, satisfying hero is composed of five layers. The same is true about an opinion paragraph.

The top of the roll is the topic sentence.
The bottom of the roll is the conclusion.
The meat is the primary support.
The cheese is the secondary support.
The lettuce and tomato are additional support.

Structure*:*

I. Topic Sentence (the top of the roll)
II. Reason No. 1 (the meat)
  A. Support (Why? So what?)
  B. Support (Specific Examples or Facts)
  C. Statistics or Personal Experience
III. Reason No. 2 (the cheese)
  A. Support
  B. Support
IV. Reason No. 3 (the lettuce and tomatoes)
  A. Support
  B. Support
V. Conclusion (the bottom of the roll)

The Writing Workout Page

OPINIONS

You are looking for a job. You go on an interview and do very well. The company offers you the position. The place operates twenty-four hours a day, seven days a week. In terms of your schedule, they are completely flexible. You may work a traditional 9:00 a.m. to 5:00 p.m. shift, or 12:00 p.m. to 8:00 p.m., 3:00 p.m. to 11:00 p.m., or even 11:00 p.m. to 7:00 a.m. You can also work weekends if you like. What time do you want to work, and why?	
Do you prefer warm weather or cold weather? Write an opinion regarding your favorite season (maybe you can describe the activities that you enjoy doing in the summer or in the winter, or you may choose to tell what kind of clothes you like to wear or your mood during the weather you like best).	

You are thinking of buying or renting a house. What kind of house do you like best? Do you like a traditional house or a modern house? What kind of house is best for you: an old comfortable house or a house with an exciting new style? Present your opinion of old versus new in the choice of a house.	
You have moved from your country to the place you live now. What's next? Do you plan to settle where you are now? Or are you thinking of moving to another place in the United States? Or else, do you want to live here for a while and then return to your country? Present your opinion on your next move in terms of living condition.	
Are you the type of person who has many friends, a wide variety of people you can talk to and socialize with? Or else do you prefer to have just a few really close friends, ones to whom you can tell all your secrets and with whom you can share all your sorrows and joys?	

Grammar in Context

COMPOUND SENTENCES AND PUNCTUATION

In the Grammar in Context section of Unit 3, we learned the difference between a sentence fragment and a complete sentence. Now we will examine how to punctuate clauses. Let's take the example of poor Nigel: *Nigel died.* We said that this was an independent clause and a complete sentence. Now let's add something:

Nigel died   Maggie cried

What sort of punctuation do we put between *Nigel died* and *Maggie cried?* We have three choices:
a. a period   b. a comma   c. no punctuation

Nigel died is an **independent clause**. *Maggie cried* is another **independent clause.** The only way to combine two independent clauses such as these is a <u>period</u>. They make two separate sentences.

Nigel died. Maggie cried.

It does not matter that the two clauses are very short. In English, we place a period between them.

Compound sentences: using conjunctions to join two independent clauses
There is another way to join two independent clauses: a conjunction. There are four basic conjunctions:

and	to add information
but, yet	for contrast
so	for a result

The compound sentence is structured in this way: SV, conjunction SV. We place a **comma** before the conjunction. The conjunction is followed by the second independent clause. Analyze the following examples:

Bob worked from 8 a.m. to 4 p.m., and he did his homework after dinner.
Silvia is excellent in tennis, and Nancy is very good at golf.
Jon doesn't study very much, but he gets good grades.
I love chocolate, but it makes me fat.
Arturo stayed up all night, yet he is not tired today.
It is a beautiful day, so we should go for a walk in the park.
You are lying, so I don't want to talk to you anymore.

Rules: 1. If there is **no** conjunction between two independent clauses, use a **period.**
2. If you use a conjunction, insert a **comma.**

Exercise 1

Insert the correct punctuation in the following sentences. Do not add any other words.

1. My sister is a doctor my brother works in a bank.
2. Jose lives in a big house so he is happy.
3. My cousin lives in China my aunt lives in Vietnam.
4. Almost everyone loves John his ex-wife does not love him.
5. Erica never smokes cigarettes her father smoked five packs a day.
6. I never drink hard liquor but on Sundays I have a glass of wine with dinner.
7. In the winter Mary goes skiing her husband and children stay home and cry.
8. My sister is very tall my brother is short.
9. Kal lives in a big city but he is unhappy.
10. Maria works very hard her brother is lazy.
11. John is a good dancer his friend Oliver is not.
12. I go to school in the morning and I work in the afternoon.
13. Sibellia usually goes to the movies on Saturday her sister usually cleans the house.
14. In the summer Young Han goes to the beach Seong Dong hates the beach.
15. At home I never wear my shoes I wear slippers in the house.
16. Carl always calls his ex-girlfriend but she does not answer the phone.
17. The weather is very cold in Minnesota in the winter the people still love to take long walks.
18. Hanna loves to hike in the woods yet she seldom does it.
19. Pluto was a planet it is not a planet anymore.
20. In the late afternoon Jose and his friends have a coffee break they do not eat anything.

Writing Assignment 1

Sample Opinion Paragraph

JANE AND HER CELL PHONE

I think my girlfriend Jane loves her new cell phone more than she loves me. When we are on dates together, she holds her phone in her palm instead of my hand. Now that I think about it, I have never once seen Jane turn her phone off or put it away. If I take her to a fancy restaurant, she will answer her phone in the middle of dinner and talk for a long time while the soup gets cold. It is very rude. In addition, her phone is pink and now she only wears pink clothes so she matches. I bought her a beautiful blue dress for her birthday, but she will not wear it because the color does not go with her phone. Last week I finally told her that I was in love with her, but she did not hear me because she was typing messages to her friends. As every day passes, I am growing more and more jealous. Because of this, I think maybe I should break up with her and try to meet a new girl who likes to talk face-to-face. I could try to meet Jane for lunch to say goodbye, but I think the only way to get her attention will be to call her.

Analyzing the paragraph:

1. What is the subject of the paragraph? ____________________

2. How does the writer feel about the subject? ____________________

   ____

   ____

3. How many reasons does the writer give to support the opinion?____________________
   List the reasons:

4. What conclusion does the writer make?____________________

5. What verb tenses are used in the paragraph? ____________________

Writing Assignment 2

Opinion Paragraphs: A Step-by-Step Process

WHY PEOPLE SHOULD STUDY ENGLISH AT YOUR COLLEGE

You are going to write an opinion paragraph using a step-by-step process. This process involves three steps:

1. **Pre-writing**: Choose a side, brainstorm reasons to support your opinion, and narrow the list.
2. **Outlining:** Prepare an idea cluster.
3. **Writing:** Follow the idea cluster to write your paragraph.

1. **Choose a side, brainstorm characteristics, and narrow the list:**
   a. First, choose a topic. For this assignment, the topic is why people should study English at your college. ______________________

   b. Now, think about the reasons why people should study English at your school. Write down up to eight of them. This process is called *brainstorming*.

   ____________________ ________________________

   ____________________ ________________________

   ____________________ ________________________

   ____________________ ________________________

   c. Read over the list. You will not need so many reasons for your opinion. You should narrow the list. Choose the best three or four. Write them here:

   ____________________ ________________________

   ____________________ ________________________

2. **Outlining: prepare an idea cluster:**
Filling out an idea cluster is an excellent way to organize your thoughts in opinion writing. Then you will be ready to write an organized paragraph. This is an idea cluster for opinion paragraphs:

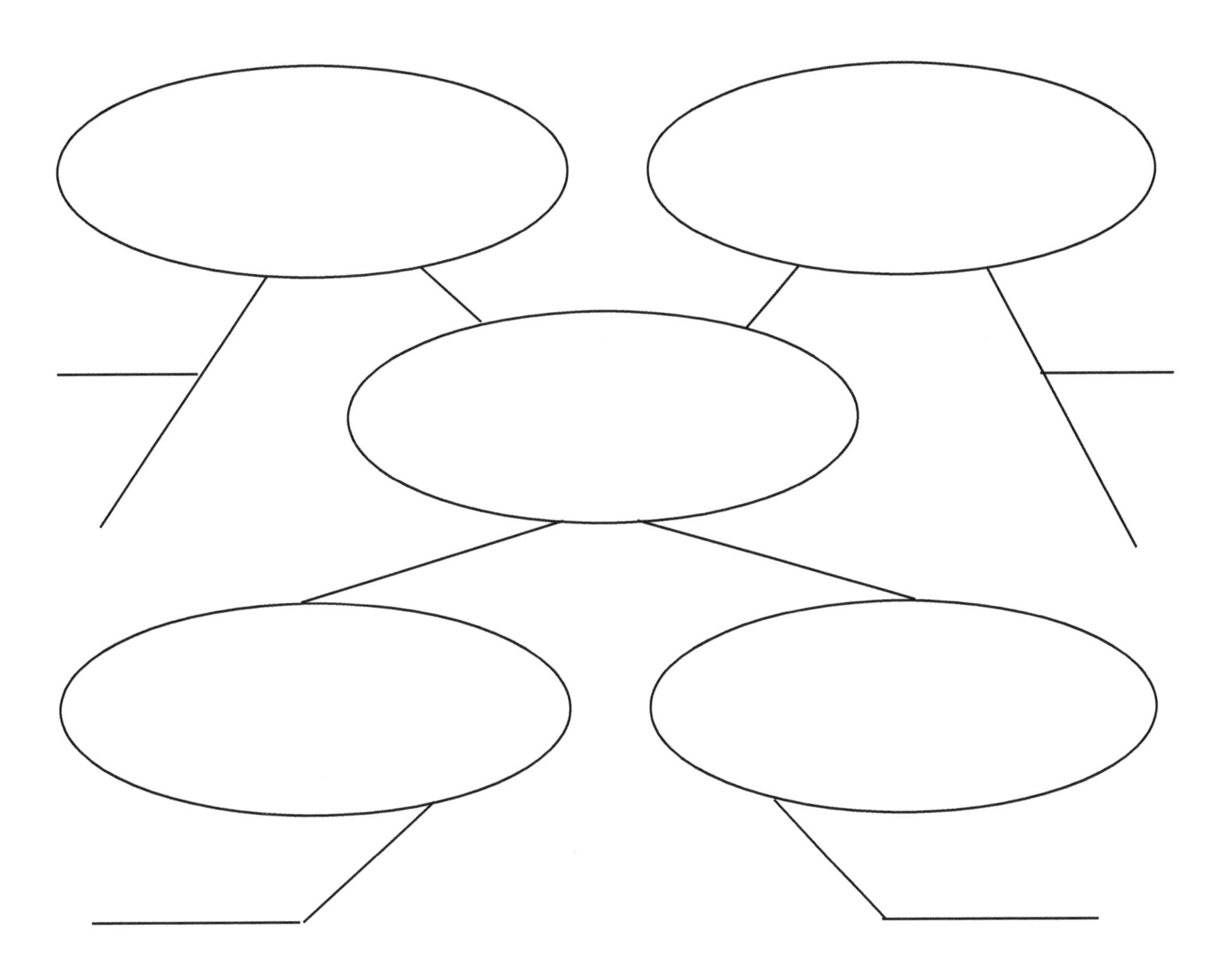

3. **Write the paragraph: Use the idea cluster to create your paragraph.**

CONSISTENCY IN SUPPORT

Notice that in the persuasion paragraph, ***all the reasons*** presented must support your point. Do not introduce points that contradict your point of view. For example, in a paragraph telling why you like fast food, you should not include a discussion of health benefits or the quality of the ingredients. You should not allow the reader (or the listener in a persuasive speech) to find weaknesses in the consistency of your support and your argument.

Tense: Simple present
Structure: List of reasons (three to four)
Discourse markers:
First, second, third, in addition, moreover
One reason is .... **Another reason is ....** **The last reason is ...**
Key words: **I think, I feel, I believe,** [that] + Subject and Verb
I think that there is too much homework in writing class.
I feel that people who cheat are only hurting themselves.
I believe that people with big noses are very lucky.

Grammar Points
When using **such as**, it is followed by a list of similar words (usually nouns, gerunds, infinitives, or the base form of the verb).

1. There are many things I have to do this weekend **such as** *clean* the house, *mow* the lawn, and *rake* the leaves.
2. I like outdoor activities **such as** *swimming, jogging*, and *hiking*.
3. He has several pets **such as** *fish, birds*, and *cats*.

When using **for example** at the start of a new sentence, it is followed by a subject and verb (an independent clause).

1. I hate people who talk too much. **For example,** *I get* really upset when my friend Natasha tells me about all her problems at work.
2. There are many things that you can do to improve your vocabulary. **For example,** *you can copy* all the new words in a separate notebook.

Writing Assignment 3

Writing about Social Issues

THE HOMELESS

Do you feel that it is the responsibility of the government to take care of homeless people? Or should the responsibility lie with the people themselves? How do you feel people become homeless? Develop a paragraph stating your opinion of homeless people.

Writing Assignment 4

Man and Woman

There are positive and negative aspects to being a man or a woman. In a clearly written, well-organized paragraph, choose one of the following topics, and give three or four reasons to support your answer.

I love being a woman for the following reasons.
I hate being a woman for the following reasons.
I love being a man for the following reasons.
I hate being a man for the following reasons.

Verb forms: Simple present
Organization: Reasons (*first*, *second*, *then*, *after that*, etc.)
Structure: According to reasons (usually three to four reasons with two to three sentences of support for each reason)

Grammar Points:

1. ***For example*** is followed by a complete sentence.
   He is impolite. ***For example,*** *he talks while other people are speaking.*
2. ***Such as*** is <u>not</u> followed by a clause, but by a short list of nouns or verbs. ***Such as*** never begins a sentence.
   There are several vegetables that I love ***such as*** *broccoli, peas, and corn.*
   I love to do many interesting things on Sunday ***such as*** *seeing a movie, talking on the phone all afternoon, and cooking excellent meals.* [remember parallel structure]

   Sentences that begin with **because** must have two clauses (D, I), with a comma after the first clause.
   Because *he is anti-social, he always eats alone.*
   If **because** is in the middle of the sentence (I D), there is **no comma**.
   He missed the class ***because*** *he was visiting his mother in jail.*

Process:

1. FIRST MAKE AN IDEA CLUSTER (IDEA MAP)
2. USE THE IDEA CLUSTER TO WRITE A PARAGRAPH

Use this structure:
Topic sentence
Reason 1
  Support
  Support (example)
Reason 2
  Support
  Support (example)
Reason 3
  Support
  Support
Conclusion

Writing Assignment 5

Gun Control Laws

THE RIGHT TO OWN A GUN

In America, according to the United States Constitution, people have the right to buy and own guns. Do you think that this is a good law? Or do you feel that only police officers and soldiers should have guns? Choose a side (in favor of citizens owning guns or against citizens owning guns) and support your opinion.

1. **List reasons to support your opinion.**

   Write three or four reasons to prove that your opinion on citizens owning guns is correct:

   ______________________________ ______________________________

   ______________________________ ______________________________

2. **Outlining: prepare an idea cluster.**
   Fill out the idea cluster with the reasons you have chosen. Don't forget to include support for your reasons.

3. **Write a paragraph.**
   Use the idea cluster to present your opinions clearly. Remember to use discourse markers to organize your paragraph into ten to twelve sentences.

Writing Assignment 6

Persuasion

FAST FOOD

There are three reasons why I do not like to eat fast food. First, I am always very careful of what I eat. I believe in eating as many natural ingredients as possible. I try to eat fruits and vegetables and not so much meat and potatoes. If you go to Kentucky Fried Chicken or Burger King, they offer almost no vegetables or fruit on the menu. Almost everything is fried and greasy. Another reason why I dislike fast food is that it makes you fat. Morgan Spurlock made a movie in 2004 called *Supersize Me.* It showed a man who ate at McDonald's every meal for a month. He gained almost 25 pounds. When you eat fast food, the number of calories is always very high. The combination of high calorie and high fat is probably very bad for your health. The third reason why I hate fast food is the price. People think that fast food is cheap, but I can cook the same food at home for much less money. There are four people in my family, and I can buy chopped meat for hamburgers, potatoes, lettuce, and tomatoes for a salad, and green beans and spinach for less than $7.00. In a fast food place, the meal would easily cost double that amount. And I know that the food I am eating is fresh because I buy it and cook it the same day. How long has the food at a fast food place been frozen? Who knows? These are the reasons why I do not like to eat fast food.

Exercises

1. Trace the structure of the persuasion paragraph, using the outline given on the previous page.

2. Underline the discourse markers (transition words) used in the paragraph.

3. Analyze the quality of the support. Has the author stated the points clearly and forcefully? Are the reasons valid? Is there anything to question in terms of the support?

Text-based writing assignment: Suppose that you were asked to write a paragraph from the *opposite point of view.* Find four reasons why you **love** fast food and provide support.

Writing Assignment 7

Success

Read the following statement:

Success means making and having a lot of money. There is no such thing as success without money. Money is the only way to measure success. The more money you have, the more successful you are.

Do you agree or disagree with this statement? Write a paragraph in which you give three reasons why you agree or disagree with the statement. First, list three or four reasons to support your decision. Then make an idea map. Finally, follow the map to write your paragraph.

Topic Sentence:

There are three reasons why I agree with the statement.

Or

There are three reasons why I disagree with the statement.

Writing Assignment 8

Punishing Children

Sometimes children behave badly. Probably at this time, their parents punish them. There are many ways to punish children when they are bad. One of them is physical. Some parents hit their children to punish them.

What do you think of this action? Is it right for parents to hit their children to punish them? Give your reaction to this question. Also, present the methods that you think parents should use to punish their children when they misbehave. You might include a summary of how parents usually punish children in your country.

1. **Write three or four reasons to support your opinion.**

   ______________________ ______________________

   ______________________ ______________________

2. **Outlining: prepare an idea cluster.**
   Fill out the idea cluster with the reasons you have chosen. Don't forget to include support for your reasons.

3. **Write a ten- to twelve-sentence paragraph.** Present your opinion clearly. Remember to use discourse markers for enumeration (*first*, *in addition*, *another reason*, *third*, *the last reason*, *finally*). Write on a separate sheet of paper.

Writing Assignment 9

Sports Fanatics

Look at the two photographs of college football fans. Describe what they look like and what they are doing. Then write an opinion paragraph on the following theme: Do you feel that Americans take sports too seriously? Are they too crazy about their teams? Or is this a healthy attitude? Cheering for a team is a normal and fun activity.

Aspen Photo/Shutterstock.com

Sean Locke Photography/Shutterstock.com

Writing Assignment 10

Journal Writing

THE ISSUE JOURNAL

The journal writing activities for opinion paragraphs is to keep an "Issue Journal." An issue is a hot topic, one that is controversial and open for discussion. The word *controversial* comes from two Latin words: *contro* meaning "against" in English, and *vers* meaning "side." For this reason, when an issue is controversial, there are two sides. One is in favor [**pro**], and the other is against [**con**]. It is possible to have two very different opinions. People can discuss and debate these issues. When you write an opinion paragraph, you try to change the mind of the other person. It is not easy to change someone's mind. But if you state your opinion clearly and forcefully, you might succeed.

In your journal writing these two weeks, state strong opinions about the following controversial issues. In some cases, you are asked to agree or disagree with the statements.

1. Music piracy: Do you think that it is wrong to download music from the internet without paying for it?

2. Should a couple live together before they get married?

3. Is cheating on tests in school acceptable? What do you do when the person next to you tries to cheat from you on a test?

4. Do you feel that athletes should be able to use steroids?

5. Should 18-year-olds be able to drink, or is the correct drinking age 21?

In your reading this week, pay particular attention to articles in newspapers, magazines, or on the internet that introduce hot issues. Read them carefully, and then provide your own opinion in a strong journal entry.

The next page provides five brief news stories on issues: punishing murderers, tattoos, owning a gun, grades in English language courses, and punishing drug possession.

The Issues Page

Smithson Executed: Shot 3 After He was Fired from Job

Roland Smithson was executed yesterday in Dallas, Texas. Four years, after he was fired from his job at Nerita Industries, he returned to the plant with a shotgun. He killed his former boss, Irene Houston, as well as three office workers. Smithson was executed by lethal injection after his appeal was denied by the Governor of Texas. Protesters against capital punishment demonstrated outside the prison. "We don't believe that it is right to execute him. His death will not bring the four people back to life."
Several members of the family of the murder victims attended the execution. "I think that he received the correct punishment," said Yosiah Houston, brother of Smithson's former manager, who was killed in her office.

Tattoo Contest Winners Declare "We Can't Wait to Get Another Tattoo!"
Audrey Maciel and Geoffrey McCloud were the winners of the "Best Tattoo" contest held last night at *Mango's* Club in South Beach, Miami, Florida. Audrey's tattoo is a heart with a three roses. It is on her left shoulder. "Each rose represents an important woman in my life: my grandmother, my mother, and my sister." Geoffrey's tattoo has the name of his girlfriend, Angela, written between two wings. His tattoo is on his left bicep. The prize in the contest is a weekend for two in Orlando, Florida, home of Disney World and Universal Studios. "I am already thinking about a new tattoo for next year's contest," said Audrey. "A tattoo is like a work of art and my body is the canvas," Geoffrey added.

Sales of Guns Rise after 9/11 Terrorist Attacks

Across the country, sales for firearms rose again for the fifth consecutive year after the terrorist attacks on the World Trade Center on September 11, 2001. In America, where it is legal to own a gun, the number of gun owners surpassed 100 million for the first time. "It is a dangerous world, and I think Americans should have the right to protect themselves," said Harlan Cabin, a postal worker from Bilouxi, Mississippi. Karen Longfellow from Lincoln, New Hampshire added, "I feel more secure knowing that I have a gun in my home, just in case." But others disagree. Anne Murray, an elementary school teacher from Santa Fe, New Mexico, warned, "I don't believe in owning guns. I think it's wrong. Look at all the accidents that happen with guns, and all the crimes that are committed with guns." "Guns kill people, and I don't believe in that, under any circumstances," explained Joseph Webber from Salt Lake City, Utah.

Grades Abolished in English Language Classes
At Baldwin College in Newton, Minnesota, international students no longer have to worry about grades in their English language courses: grades have been abolished. Students will receive only Pass or Fail grades. "This way students can concentrate only on learning, without the worry of test scores and final grades," explained Rose Bo, director of the English language program. Roger Aps, who teaches English at Baldwin, noted, "If you take the stress of grades out of the process, students will probably learn more." Not everyone agrees, most notably many students. "I study very hard, and I feel very satisfied when I get an A," said Rodrigo Gonzalez, from Ecuador. "For me, it's fine," according to Daniela Rudd from Ukraine. "I can concentrate only on learning English, without worrying.

Woman Sentenced to One Year for Drug Possession
Katie Hughes, 26, was sentenced to one year in prison for possession of 450 grams of marijuana. "It's ridiculous," said Ms. Hughes' mother Hilary. "That's a long time in jail for a small amount of drugs." The penalty was part of a mandatory sentencing program put in place last year in Ohio. "They should use jails for real criminals," added Hilary.

JOURNAL ENTRIES

Read the news stories on the previous page, and write journal entries in which you present your opinion:

1. How do you feel murderers should be punished for their crime?

2. How do you feel about tattoos? Do you have one or would you ever consider getting one?

3. Do you feel that the world is a much more dangerous place after the events of September 11, 2001? Why or why not?

4. Do you think that all grades in English language courses should have Pass / Fail grades instead of regular A, B, C, D, and F grades?

5. In your opinion, what is the correct punishment for the possession of small quantities of drugs?

CHAPTER 8

Block Structure

(BACK AND FORTH ORDER)

UNIT 1: MAKING COMPARISONS
UNIT 2: CAUSE AND EFFECT

UNIT 1: MAKING COMPARISONS

- The food in Thailand is spicier than the food in America.
- People walk faster in New York than in Miami.
- Seoul is more crowded than Dallas.
- Prada shoes are more expensive than Timberlands.
- My friend Josefa is neater than my friend Nestor.

These are all comparison sentences. You see *differences* between two things all the time. Especially when you first came to the United States, you probably compared everything in America with your country. The food was different, the people were different, and the lifestyle was different. When you organize your discussion about the differences between two things, you write *comparison paragraphs.*

PARAGRAPH CHART FOR MAKING COMPARISONS

Verb forms used	1. Usually simple present tense *My brother John is lazier than my brother Phil.* 2. Simple past for specific examples *Yesterday John* ***worked*** *until 11:00 p.m. On the other hand, Maria* ***finished*** *at 6:00 p.m.*
Objects of comparison	The *objects of comparison* are the two things that you are comparing, such as your brothers John and Phil. You could also compare two cities, two movies, two restaurants, or two watches.
Points of comparison	The *points of comparison* are the **differences** between the two objects of comparison. For example, in a comparison of two watches, the points of comparison might be price, quality, and style.
Organization	There are two possible structures: 1. ***Direct comparison***. In this method, you go back and forth between the two objects of comparison. *Miami has many outdoor dance clubs. Boston's clubs are all indoors.* *Maya gets up at 5:00 a.m. on Sundays while Jose loves to sleep in.* 2. ***Separated structure***. When you use separated structure, you write everything about one of the objects of comparison. Then you write a transition (*on the other hand)*, followed by the information about the other object of comparison. For example: *Many of Miami's clubs are outdoors. People can dance under the stars and enjoy the cool breeze. It is very romantic. After dancing, people can take a walk on Ocean Drive in South Beach.* *On the other hand, Boston's clubs are all indoors. In many months, the weather is too cold to stay outside. The atmosphere is typical of clubs in northern cities. After dancing, people get into their cars and drive to restaurants, diners, or cafes. Or some go directly home.*
Discourse markers	*One difference is, another difference is, the last difference is* **Contrast words**: *but, yet, however, nevertheless, nonetheless, although, while, on the other hand*
Topic sentence	1. There are many differences between _____ and _____. 2. My two friends Ashraf and Ihab are very different.

Concluding sentence	You do not have to choose between the two objects of comparison or tell which or whom you prefer (*I love my brother Phil, but I hate my brother John.*). Simply discuss the last point of comparison.
Grammar points	Study the ways to write comparison sentences: 1. **Independent clause, comma, conjunction, independent clause** *Joan studies hard, but Nancy never does her homework.* *Roger has an old car, but Leo's car is brand new.* *It seldom rains in Arizona, yet Lynn's garden is lush.* 2. **Independent clause, semicolon, conjunction, comma, independent clause.** *Min is 7'3" tall; however, he doesn't play basketball.* *Sue left early for the concert; nevertheless, she arrived late.* *Rodolfo is a terrible dancer; nonetheless, he goes to clubs every Saturday night.* 3. **Conjunction, dependent clause, comma, independent clause** *Although Jim lives 100 miles away, we still see each other every weekend.* *While some people like to eat a big breakfast, others only drink a cup of coffee.* *Though Irena speaks four languages, she cannot communicate with her mother.* 4. **Independent clause (no punctuation) dependent clause.** *Dorothy loves jogging while Karen hates it.* *I never get an A although I study a lot.* *Javier bought a new pair of pants and a party shirt though he really doesn't need them.*

Grammar in Context

COMPLEX SENTENCES

We have already studied *simple* sentences and *compound* sentences. Now it is time to analyze the last sentence type, *complex* sentences. A complex sentence has two clauses, one **independent** and one **dependent**. There are two possible combinations:

Dependent + Independent
Independent + Dependent

Let's analyze each of them:

1. The first type of complex sentence is more common. The sentence begins with a coordinating conjunction followed by the subject and verb. A comma goes in the middle of the sentence. Then there is another subject and verb. The formula is:

   Conjunction SV, SV.

   The first clause is dependent. The second clause is independent.

   Although Henrietta eats a lot, she is very thin.
   (conj) (subject) (verb) , (s) (v)
   [dependent clause] [independent clause]

   Notice that the following sentences have two clauses: the first clause is dependent and the second clause is independent.

   Because it was raining, Toshiko stayed home.
   After Bobbie cleaned the kitchen floor, he cooked dinner.
   If you get home before 10, you should call me.
   Although Jim has heavy legs, he is a very fast runner.

   Because introduces a result clause. *After* begins a time clause. *If* starts a conditional clause. *Although* introduces contrast.

2. We may switch the order of the two clauses in a complex sentence. We can begin with an *independent* clause and end with a *dependent* clause. The formula is:

   SV conjunction SV.

   Notice that there is <u>no comma</u> in the middle of this kind of sentence.

Cornelia feels very sad because she misses her friends.
(Subject)(verb) *(conj)* *S* *V*
[independent clause] *[dependent clause]*

We will have a party when Marta and Carlos have their baby.
I still love you although you are a liar.
Mark eats in inexpensive restaurants because he has little money.
Teresa will help you if you ask her.

Complex sentences for contrast

In this unit, we write complex sentences to discuss contrast. We use two common coordinating conjunctions: **although** and **while**. Let's see how a sentence is constructed. We begin with a dependent clause:

Although Phyllis is rich

The connotation of the clause is *positive*: it is good to be rich. However, because the sentence begins with the word **although,** we know that something negative is coming up. The second clause is independent, and it will be a surprise.

Although Phyllis is rich, *she doesn't spend a dime.*

Because Phyllis has a lot of money, you expect her to buy many things, eat out all the time, and go to shows and concerts. You expect her to be generous. However, she holds on to her money, which is a surprising thing.

The word **while** is also used in contrast sentences. It has a different meaning than when we use it in time clauses (*While I was taking a shower, I sang the latest Shakira song.*). In contrast clauses, **while** is used for *direct opposites*. We begin with a dependent clause:

While Victor is a pessimist

This clause has a *negative* connotation. Victor has a negative view of life. In the second clause, we have to introduce an opposite idea, usually with a different person.

While Victor is a pessimist, *Lina is an optimist.*

The second clause is *positive*. Victor and Lina have opposite attitudes. Here are a few other examples with *although* and *while.*

Although Susanna is from the Philippines, she has blond hair.
While my sister has a large house, my brother lives in a studio apartment.
Although gas is expensive, people continue to buy large SUVs.
While Joe works 9 to 5, his friend Hal works the graveyard shift (11 to 7).

Complex sentences for contrast may also follow the other formula (SV **conjunction** SV):

Maureen has a lot of money in the bank although her salary is not high.
Rose loves opera while Hank finds it boring.
The food was terrible, but I still ate everything.

GRAMMAR EXERCISES

Exercise 1
Complete the sentence with an appropriate independent clause.

1. Because Sandra loves grammar class, ______________________________.
2. Although Sun Hye lives close to school, ______________________________.
3. If you need my help, ______________________________.
4. While my brother is very tall, ______________________________.
5. When Olivia passed the nursing examination, ______________________________.

Exercise 2
Punctuate the following sentences.

1. While my father loves spicy food my mother hates it.
2. Although Nick runs very slowly he is an excellent defender in soccer.
3. Sal will pick up little Joey from preschool if you don't get back in time.
4. I love you because you always help me with my homework.
5. Because the weather was so bad they cancelled the trip to the museum.

Comparison Chart 1: Analyze the following chart.

Marcia	Her sister Hilda
high salary lives in a contemporary house very tall outgoing an optimist	low salary lives in a very old house short shy a realist

Exercise 3

Write five contrast sentences based on the information in the chart.

1. While Marcia …
2. Although Hilda is …
3. While Marcia …
4. Marcia is _______ while Hilda is _______.
5. Marcia lives _______ although Hilda _______.

Exercise 4

Write five sentences comparing two of your relatives. Use *although* and *while.*

1.
2.
3.
4.
5.

ADJECTIVES: DESCRIPTION, COMPARATIVE, SUPERLATIVE, AND EQUATIVE FORMS

Adjectives have four forms. The *descriptive* form is used to describe one noun or pronoun. Remember that adjectives are placed immediately before the noun or after the be-verb:

*We visited a **beautiful** beach.*
*The tree is **tall** and **shady**.*
*Carl's **little** sister is **energetic**.*

The *comparative* form is used to compare two nouns or pronouns. For short adjectives, add *-er*. For longer adjectives (more than two syllables), use *more* + adjective. The adjectives are followed by *than*.

*Keira is **taller** than her mother.*
*Nancy is **older** than her husband.*
*Jackson is more **intelligent** than his boss.*

The *superlative* form of the adjective is used to compare at least three nouns or pronouns. For short adjectives, add *the* + *est*. For longer adjectives (more than two syllables), use *the* + *most* + adjective. The adjectives are followed by *in*.

*Isabella is **the youngest** architect in the company.*
*Ronaldo is **the fastest** player in the league.*
*Edyta is **the most** intelligent student in the school.*

The *equative* form and the *non-equative* form are used to express equality or inequality. Use *as* + adjective + *as* or *not as* + adjective + *as* to make this form.

*Marion is **as fast as** John.*
*Jason is **as fat as** his father.*
*Rosa is **not as tall as** Cinzia.*
*Rome is **not as crowded as** Tokyo.*

Remember the forms of *good*:

Descriptive: good	Comparative: better	
Superlative: best	Equative: as good as	Non-equative: not as good as

*Daniel is a **good** swimmer.*
*Olga is a **better** dancer than Leila.*
*Sheila is the **best** singer in the choir.*
*He is **as good as** his brother.*
*The Nile Restaurant is **not as good as** The Four Seasons.*

Comparison Chart 2: Analyze the following chart.

Helga	46 years old	5' 11" tall	Very organized	gets As	17 pairs of shoes
Rosa	46 years old	5' 10" tall	Organized	gets Cs	21 pairs of shoes
Irina	41 years old	5' 6" tall	Very messy	gets Bs	17 pairs of shoes

Exercise 5
Write three sentences with the *descriptive* form (i.e., Helga is … . Irina has …).

1.

2.

3.

Exercise 6
Write three sentences with the *comparative* form (*-er* + *than*, or *more* + adjective + *than*).

1.

2.

3.

Exercise 7
Write three sentences with the *superlative* form (*the* + *-est*, or *the most* + adjective).

1.

2.

3.

Exercise 8
Write three sentences with the *equative* and *non-equative* form (*as* + adjective + *as*; *not as* + adjective + *as* (i.e., as tall as; not as lazy as).

1.

2.

3.

Comparison Chart 3: Analyze the following chart comparing three U.S. states.

New Jersey	9,000,000 people	Polluted	Small	Many beaches	Many jobs	No mountains
Wyoming	500,000 people	Very clean	Very large	No beaches	Some jobs	High mountains
New Hampshire	800,000 people	Very clean	Small	Some beaches	Not too many jobs	Low mountains

Exercise 9

Write three sentences with the *descriptive* form (i.e., New Jersey is…; Wyoming has…).

1.

2.

3.

Exercise 10

Write three sentences with the *comparative* form (*-er* + *than*, or *more* + adjective + *than*).

1.

2.

3.

Exercise 11

Write three sentences with the *superlative* form (*the* + *-est*, or *the most* + adjective).

1.

2.

3.

Exercise 12

Write three sentences with the *equative* and *non-equative* form (*as* + adjective + *as*; *not as* + adjective + *as* (i.e., as rich as; not as intelligent as).

1.

2.

3.

The Writing Workout Page

COMPARISON WRITING

When you finish school, you might begin your working career or change from your current job. You will probably not start as the president or chief executive officer in the company. As a result, you will have a boss. Write a comparison between a good boss and a bad boss. What characteristics does a good manager have? How would you talk about the personality and behavior of a bad boss?	
Now you will discuss movies. Write about the types of movies that you really like. Tell why you like these kinds of movies. Then compare it with the movies that you don't enjoy at all. (For example: *I love action/adventure films because they make me excited, but I don't like romantic comedies because I think they are stupid.*)	
For a long vacation, do you prefer to drive or to fly? Discuss some of the good and bad points about these two methods of traveling.	

You are moving into a new apartment. It is empty, totally empty. It is your job to fill it up with furniture and other items. Are you the type of person who loves to put many things in the apartment: furniture, paintings, statues, photographs, and souvenirs? Or instead, do you prefer to leave the place bare, with only the necessary minimum? Talk about the two styles of decoration.	
Some people love antiques. They enjoy being surrounded by old things. They like the sense of history in the objects: grandma's furniture, old magazines and books, classic cars, even old music. On the other hand, there are other types of people. They love everything new: new furniture, new clothes, new cars, and new music. What type of person are you? Compare the two attitudes: old or new for you?	

Writing Assignment 1

Brainstorming and Organizing Comparisons

1. *Brainstorm*: When you are given a topic for comparison, the first step is to **brainstorm differences**. Think about the topic for a few minutes. Then write as many differences as you can in two minutes. Do not stop to analyze or reject any differences. Simply write them down.

    ______________________　　　　______________________

    ______________________　　　　______________________

    ______________________　　　　______________________

    ______________________　　　　______________________

2. *Narrow the differences*. Choose the **four differences** that are richest in possibilities for discussion. You will probably need only three differences for your paragraph, but keep the fourth in reserve in case you find that you have not written enough. These differences will be your ***points of comparison.***

    ______________________　　　　______________________

    ______________________　　　　______________________

3. *Set up a comparison chart.* Enter the points of comparison in the first vertical column on the left and the ***objects of comparison*** (the two things that you are comparing) at the top of the other two columns.

4. *Add the details.* Add as much information as you can to fill in the chart.

5. *Write the paragraph.* Follow the comparison chart closely to write the comparison paragraph.

POINTS OF COMPARISON	OBJECT OF COMPARISON 1	OBJECT OF COMPARISON 2
Point of Comparison 1 (the first difference)		
Point of Comparison 2 (the second difference)		
Point of Comparison 3 (the third difference)		
Point of Comparison 4 (the fourth difference, if necessary)		

Writing Assignment 2

Comparing Two Members of Your Family

First, fill out the chart. Then write an eleven-sentence paragraph comparing your mother and your father, or two brothers or sisters, or two grandparents.

Follow this procedure:

1. Brainstorm the differences between the two individuals.

   1. 2. 3. 4. 5.

   6. 7. 8. 9. 10.

2. Narrow the differences by choosing the four best differences.

   1. 2. 3. 4.

3. Set up a comparison chart.

	Relative 1 ( )	Relative 2 ( )
Difference 1 ( )		
Difference 2 ( )		
Difference 3 ( )		
Difference 4 ( )		

4. Follow the comparison chart and write a paragraph on a separate sheet of paper.

Structure:

1. Topic Sentence
2. Point of comparison 1
   - Person 1
   - Person 2
3. Point of comparison 2
   - Person 1
   - Person 2
4. Point of comparison 3
   - Person 1
   - Person 2
5. Conclusion

© Brian J. Altano

At-home writing assignment: Comparing two types of music

1. Brainstorm the differences between the two types of music.

   1. 2. 3. 4. 5.

   6. 7. 8. 9. 10.

2. Narrow the differences by choosing the best three.

   1. 2. 3.

3. Set up a comparison chart. Fill in the chart. Then write a paragraph comparing two types of music.

POINTS OF COMPARISON	OBJECT 1: PERSON 1	OBJECT 2: PERSON 2
Difference 1:		
Difference 2:		
Difference 3:		

Writing Assignment 3

Comparing Residences

In this paragraph you will compare your apartment (or house) in the United States where you live now with your apartment (or house) in your native country.

Follow this procedure:

1. Brainstorm the differences between the two residences.

1.	2.	3.	4.	5.
6.	7.	8.	9.	10.

2. Narrow the differences by choosing the best three.

1.	2.	3.

3. Make a comparison chart.

	YOUR APARTMENT OR HOUSE IN THE UNITED STATES	YOUR APARTMENT OR HOUSE IN YOUR NATIVE COUNTRY
Difference 1:		
Difference 2:		
Difference 3:		

4. Follow the comparison chart to write a paragraph on a separate sheet of paper.

Writing Assignment 4

Going on Vacation

THE MOUNTAINS, THE BEACH, THE CITY

When it comes to vacation, there are "mountain people," "beach people," and "city people." Usually people prefer one of these places the most. Some like to hike, commune with nature, and enjoy the fresh air. Others like the intense sun and warm water of the shore, wearing only a bathing suit and suntan lotion. Other people prefer to travel to cities on vacation, to visit museums, shows, restaurants, and clubs.

© Theo Solomon

Iakov Kalinin/Shutterstock.com

© Theo Solomon

What sort of person are you? When you choose a vacation, do you prefer the mountains, the beach, or the city? Give the reasons why you love your favorite destination. Then describe the perfect vacation.

Writing Assignment 5

Description Writing

A PIECE OF CHOCOLATE CAKE

Let's analyze a simple piece of chocolate cake with icing. The ingredients of the cake are flour, sugar, cocoa powder, butter, baking soda, and vanilla. The ingredients of the icing are butter, heavy cream, sour cream, sugar, and cocoa. A slice of this chocolate cake has 454 calories. The icing adds another 212, for a total of 666 calories. The cake and icing have 36 grams of fat and 142 grams of carbohydrates. Is it the perfect dessert? Is it the end of a fantastic meal? Or is it a diet disaster? Is it a guilty pleasure that is equivalent to sin?

The way that people view a piece of chocolate cake might depend on their culture. Many Americans consider the cake with guilt. They see it as a prohibited object. Chocolate cake is not in any diet book. However, Americans indulge. They cut a large slice of cake. They eat it. They eat it all up. They eat it very quickly, almost as if their mother or their boss is watching them. There is not a morsel left. They even scrape the rest of the icing from the plate. First, they smile. Then they begin to feel terrible. The cake is good, but it is also bad. Americans might punish themselves for eating the cake. Perhaps they will not eat breakfast the next day. They might walk an extra mile during their next workout session. But one thing is for sure: many Americans feel guilty about the cake. For many of them, it is a sign of weakness. They have given in to the temptation of something delicious, but which is perhaps bad for them.

On the other hand, French people eat the same piece of chocolate cake. However, they do not feel guilty. They consider the chocolate cake as a reward after a hard day. They *deserve* the cake. They cut a regular size slice of cake. They eat it slowly. They close their eyes and enjoy the pleasure of the wonderful flavor of the chocolate, cream, and butter. They indulge. They do not feel that they are giving in to weakness. It is good, completely good. They discuss the quality of the cake in groups. They travel extra miles to go to a pastry shop with the best chocolate cake.

Many Koreans look at the chocolate cake with interest. It is an exotic item. Chocolate is not a common part of the Asian diet. They try the cake, eating a very small slice. It is sweet, maybe too sweet. Sweet foods are rarer in Korean cooking than in French or American cooking. They feel neither pleasure nor guilt about the cake. It is simply a dessert, and they are content with this nice end to a good meal.

Choose the correct answer to the following questions:

1. The strongest attitude of Americans towards chocolate cake is probably:
    a. guilt.
    b. pleasure.
    c. hate.
    d. love.

2. The word *morsel* in the second paragraph means:
   a. crumb.
   b. big piece.
   c. leftover cake.
   d. chocolate.

3. The discourse marker *On the other hand*, which begins the third paragraph, serves what purpose?
   a. to introduce a contrast
   b. to add more information
   c. to show a result
   d. to introduce a new topic

4. The strongest attitude of the French toward chocolate cake is probably:
   a. guilt.
   b. pleasure.
   c. hate.
   d. love.

5. The number of calories in the icing on chocolate cake is:
   a. 666.
   b. 454.
   c. 212.
   d. 142.

6. The number of grams of carbohydrates in the chocolate cake is:
   a. 666.
   b. 454.
   c. 212.
   d. 142.

7. The total number of calories in the chocolate cake is:
   a. 666.
   b. 454.
   c. 212.
   d. 142.

8. The connotation of the word *prohibited* ("they see it as a prohibited object") is:
   a. positive.
   b. negative.
   c. neutral.

9. The connotation of the word *weakness* is:
   a. positive.
   b. negative.
   c. neutral.

10. The connotation of the word *indulge* is:
    a. positive.
    b. negative.
    c. neutral.

11. We can infer from the reading that many Americans:
    a. work out.
    b. do not work out.
    c. never eat chocolate cake.
    d. do not like French food.

12. We can infer from the reading that the French feel all the following emotions when they eat chocolate cake EXCEPT:
    a. pleasure.
    b. guilt.
    c. joy.
    d. contentment.

13. The connotation of the word *exotic* is:
    a. positive.
    b. negative.
    c. neutral.

14. Who eats the largest slice of cake?
    a. Koreans
    b. the French
    c. Americans

15. Who feels the most guilt after eating a slice of cake?
    a. Koreans
    b. the French
    c. Americans

16. Who considers chocolate cake something foreign and exotic?
    a. Koreans
    b. the French
    c. Americans

17. Who feels that they deserve the chocolate cake after a hard day?
    a. Koreans
    b. the French
    c. Americans

18. The Korean attitude toward chocolate cake is:
    a. pleasure.
    b. guilt.
    c. joy.
    d. contentment.

Text-based writing assignment: In a clearly written, well-organized paragraph, describe how you feel about a piece of rich, creamy, buttery chocolate cake. Also include your feelings about other very rich foods.

Writing Assignment 6

Comparison Paragraph

THE WEST EDMONTON MALL AND THE MALL OF AMERICA

(1) Two malls in North America are among the largest in the world. The West Edmonton Mall is near the city of Edmonton in the province of Alberta, Canada and the Mall of America is in Bloomington in the state of Minnesota, in the U.S. The size of these two malls is incredible. The West Edmonton Mall is larger, with 5.3 million square feet of space. The Mall of America has an area of 4.2 million square feet. Both malls are primarily shopping places. The West Edmonton Mall (WEM) has 800 stores while the Mall of America (MOA) has 520. They both have many restaurants, too: 110 for the WEM and 51 for the MOA.

(2) Both malls have plenty of entertainment, too. The WEM has 26 movie screens to 14 screens for the MOA. At the West Edmonton Mall, there is an indoor water park, an ice skating rink, and submarine rides. The WEM even has a Las Vegas–style casino for adults and Rock 'n Ride Dance Party for teenagers. The MOA also offers many attractions. It has the NASCAR Silicon Motor Speedway and Legoland. There are three roller coasters and a large Ferris wheel. Underwater Adventures Aquarium presents spectacular fish from around the world. There is a church (The River Church at Mall of America) and even a wedding chapel called The Chapel of Love, where people can get married.

(3) The Mall of America opened in 1992. The MOA is located on the former site of Metropolitan Stadium, where the Minnesota Vikings played football and the Minnesota Twins played baseball until new stadiums were built. Many people arrive at the mall by car. There are 20,000 parking spaces; 13,000 of these spaces are in two seven-storey garages at the north and south ends of the building. The MOA is also the center of a large transportation hub. Busses and trains connect the mall and Minneapolis–St. Paul (the Twin Cities), as well as the airport and other major towns. Every year, more than 40 million people visit the Mall of America.

(4) The West Edmonton Mall was built in four phases, from 1981 to 1998. It is now the largest entertainment and shopping center in the world. The WEM has the same number of parking spaces as the MOA: 20,000. Trains and busses also connect the mall with the two largest cities in the area: Edmonton and Calgari. Visitors who wish to stay overnight can book a room at the Fantasyland Hotel or sleep in one of three campgrounds located within 15 minutes of the mall. More than 30 million visitors walk through WEM's 58 entrances annually. It is open 365 days a year.

(5) Both malls offer plenty of jobs. About 23,500 people work at the WEM, which is located in the western end of Edmonton, a city of almost 1 million inhabitants. The MOA employs almost 20,000 workers. It is located in Bloomington, Minnesota, a city with 85,000 inhabitants. It is 15 minutes from Minneapolis–St. Paul. Although there are many differences between the WEM and the MOA, one item is identical. The two malls have the same owner: the *Triple Five Group*, directed by the Ghermezian brothers of Canada. And because they are almost 2,000 miles apart, there is certainly no competition for customers.

Listing differences and similarities

List four differences between MOA and WEM.

1.

2.

3.

4.

List four similarities between the two malls.

1.

2.

3.

4.

Scanning for facts

Scan (read for specific information) the article on the two malls, and fill in the following information.

1. The number of stores in the MOA: ____________________
2. The number of parking spaces at the WEM: ______________
3. How many people work at the WEM? ___________________
4. How many movie screens are there at the MOA? ___________
5. Who owns the WEM? _________________
6. Who owns the MOA? _________________
7. How many restaurants are there at the WEM? ____________
8. How many people visit the MOA each year? _____________
9. What sort of entertainment is offered at the MOA? ________________________________

   ____
10. What sort of entertainment is offered at the WEM? ________________________________

    ____

Analyzing the structure

Reread the five paragraphs. Tell which structure is used within each paragraph. Write *S* for separated structure and *D* for direct comparison.

Paragraph 1: _______

Paragraph 2: _______

Paragraph 3: _______

Paragraph 4: _______

Paragraph 5: _______

Text-based writing assignment: Write a paragraph in which you compare two places. If you live in a busy shopping area, you might compare two malls. Otherwise, compare two individual stores, two restaurants, or two parks. Try to find both differences and similarities.

Writing Assignment 7

Diary Entries

DEAR DIARY: A ROCKY ROAD TO LOVE

Zara Haddad and Alexon Kevorkian both kept a diary for almost fifteen years. Here are four entries from each of their diaries. The first entry is from 1986 and the last is from 2004. The entries discuss basically the same events However, the descriptions vary because of the different points of view.

The Diary of Zara Haddad

Dear Diary: **January 14, 1986**
I am the most miserable woman in the world. Today I have to break up with my boyfriend Alexon. I am 19 years old and the only daughter in my family. I have three older brothers. My parents are very old-fashioned and really strict. They hate my boyfriend. They tell me the reasons every day. First of all, he has a different religion. Second, he comes from a different country. Finally, they say that he is "not serious enough." He is in college, but he is still undecided about his future. He is twenty-four years old. I think he is very intelligent and handsome. He is really sweet, and I like him a lot. I don't know if I love him yet. But every time I come home, my parents yell at me. I can't take it anymore. I have to break up with him to have peace at home.

Dear Diary: **February 11, 1991**
Today I went to an Armenian church. I didn't go to hear mass or to listen to the priest. I went to see a wedding. I hid in the back of the church because I was not invited. I wore a heavy coat with a high collar, a big hat, and a black scarf that covered half my face. I did not want anyone to recognize me. It was Alexon's wedding day. Today he married a pretty woman named Olga. She walked into the church with a beautiful white dress and the organ played nice music. Alexon was waiting for her. He looked older, but he was still handsome. He looked happy. At one point, when the bride was walking down the aisle, I think he noticed me. He stared in my direction for a long time. Then at the last minute he looked at the bride and turned away. I felt cold and hot. My head was spinning. I didn't stay much after that. I left the church crying.

Dear Diary: **June 17, 1996**
Today was an excellent day. I got a promotion at the bank. I became a Vice-President. I really like my job, and Chase Manhattan Bank is a great place to work. I am in the auditing department. I get to travel, too. I go to Seoul, Taipei, Tokyo, and Kuala Lumpur. Traveling is very exciting. I am very happy with my apartment in Manhattan. It is very small, only two tiny rooms. And I have to walk up to the fifth floor. There is no elevator in the building. But the apartment is on Third Avenue and 28th Street. What a wonderful neighborhood! There are people outside all the time, and I feel very safe. Tomorrow I will join a health club in the building next to my apartment. I want to work out. I have not gained any weight since I was 19, but I want to have more energy. I will try to exercise three times a week. I am dating a few men, but I must admit that I still think of Alexon every once in a while. I wonder what he is doing.

Dear Diary: **September 9, 2004**

Sometimes the most incredible things happen! I was at the gym working out today. I was on a treadmill walking for 30 minutes. There are many treadmills in a row, at least fifteen. I looked at the treadmill next to me. Guess who was standing there? Yes, it was Alexon. He looked at me. Then he looked again. Then he started smiling. I stopped running and got off the treadmill. I went over to him and gave him a hug. He was a little different. He was a little chubby, and he was losing his hair. The hair on the side of his head, near his temples, was a little gray. But when I looked into his eyes, it was the same old Alexon. He didn't stop smiling at me. He told me that I looked beautiful. He invited me for a cup of coffee after our workout. I didn't know what to say or how to feel. But I said yes. We went to a small place on the next block. He asked me everything about myself. I told him about my life, my studies, my job, and my apartment. He explained about his life. He told me that his marriage only lasted five years. Alexon's wife found another man, and left with him. Then Alexon went back to school and studied art. He became an illustrator for children's books. He is living in Manhattan, too, on the Upper West Side. He said that he found a new job in this neighborhood. That's why he joined my health club. What an incredible coincidence! I don't know what to think or how to feel. Was it fate that brought us together again? Who knows? Anyway, I am going to have dinner with him on Saturday night. After that, who can tell?

The Diary of Alexon Kevorkian

Dear Diary: **January 15, 1986**

I don't understand what happened today. I called my girlfriend Zara and asked her what time she wanted me to come to take her out. She said seven o'clock. She told me she had something serious to talk to me about. I saw her and immediately knew there was trouble. She explained to me that her parents did not like me. They were not happy that I had a different religion. They want me to have a good job with a good salary. But now I am only a student, and I live with my sister. I am not lazy, but I don't know exactly what I want to do with my life. There is one thing I do know. I love Zara. However, she told me that she doesn't want to see me anymore. She was tired of her parents and all their complaints about me. I told her to think it over. Maybe she will change her mind. I am really angry at her parents. How can they do this to us?

Dear Diary: **February 11, 1991**

It is very strange to write a diary on my wedding night. But today something strange happened. I was in church to get married. I was waiting for Olga, my bride, to walk down the aisle. I looked around the church at all the guests. And in the back of the church I saw a beautiful woman. I swear that it was Zara. She had on a big coat with the collar turned up, a big black hat, and a thick scarf that covered half her face. But I could see her eyes. I knew it was her. I felt a pain in my heart. I wanted to run down the aisle to talk to her. But, of course, that was ridiculous. I kept looking at her. Then I noticed that Olga was right next to me. The music was playing, and her father shook my hand. Five minutes later, I looked to the back of the church. There was no one there. Maybe I was dreaming. Maybe it was not Zara. I can't tell. But tonight I feel very strange. I love Olga, but I still think of Zara almost every day. Oh well …

Dear Diary: **October 9, 1996**

Today Olga told me that our marriage was over. She told me that she didn't love me. She loved someone else. I don't know what to think. She left this evening with a suitcase. She will come back next week to get her stuff. Our marriage was not so happy. I think I will go back to school to finish my degree. I have been working at a terrible job in a film-processing plant. The pay is good, but the work is really boring and repetitive. I do the same thing every day. I think I want to study illustration. I want to work on my drawing skills. I feel very empty about the end of my marriage. I wanted it to be great, but it never was. Now I am alone. I wonder where Zara is. I still think of her at least once a day. So many years have passed, more than ten. She probably does not even remember me. I feel so lonely.

Dear Diary: **September 9, 2004**

Today was like a dream. I started a new job last week. It is my first job as an illustrator. It took me four years to get my degree in illustration. Then I looked for a job all summer. Finally I found one. I do illustrations for children's books. It is a really interesting job. Everybody is very creative. That's not the best thing about today, though. Going to school and eating in the cafeteria every day and eating junk food for supper made me a little fat. So I joined a health club. Today I went for the first time. I walked around looking at all the machines. Then I decided to go on a treadmill to begin my workout. I looked at the woman running very fast next to me. I couldn't believe it! It was Zara! She looked the same as when we were together. She looked fantastic! I can't describe how happy I was to see her. She came over to me and gave me a hug. I didn't know what to say. I couldn't even talk. I just smiled and smiled. She is an auditor for Chase Manhattan Bank. She travels all around the world. I always knew that she was incredibly intelligent. She has a great job. She lives in this neighborhood, one block from the health club. I asked her out for a cup of coffee. When I looked at her, I felt fantastic. I told her about my studies and my job. We talked and talked at the coffee shop. I couldn't stop looking at her. What a coincidence meeting her! Maybe somebody up there likes me. I can't wait to see her again. We are going out to dinner on Saturday night. We have so many things to talk about. I hope she still likes me a little. I can't stop thinking about her. Saturday seems like such a long time away. Who knows what the future holds?

Analyzing the text

True or false. Write (T) or (F) before the sentence. If the sentence is false, change the wrong parts to make it true.

1. _____ Zara and Alexon get married on February 11, 1991.
2. _____ Zara is an illustrator of children's books.
3. _____ Alexon gets married but then gets divorced five years later.
4. _____ Zara gets married but then gets divorced five years later.
5. _____ Zara has a great job with Chase Manhattan Bank.
6. _____ Zara has gained weight since 1986, but not Alexon.
7. _____ Alexon lives near the health club where he and Zara meet.
8. _____ Alexon gets his degree in illustration in 1991.
9. _____ Zara's parents love Alexon because he has a great personality and a great job.
10. _____ Zara never thinks of Alexon, but he often thinks of her.

Finishing the thought

Complete the sentences.

1. When Alexon looks to the back of the church during his wedding ...
2. Zara begins to work out because ...
3. Alexon goes back to school and ...
4. Alexon gets a job ...
5. Zara travels ...
6. Zara's position is ...
7. In 1991 ...
8. Zara breaks up with Alexon because ...
9. At a health club on Third and 28th ...
10. On the Saturday night after they meet at the health club ...

Text-Based Writing Assignment: Making Projections

Write two journals, one for Zara Haddad and one for Alexon Kevorkian. The date of the journal is September 10, 2006. Tell what happened to them in the two years since the last journal. Write the journal from the points of view of Zara and Alexon.

Dear Diary **September 10, 2006** **(written by Zara)**

Dear Diary **September 10, 2006** **(written by Alexon)**

Writing Skills: Understanding Different Perspectives

Write a diary entry from the perspective of Zara's parents. Tell why they want her to break up with Alexon. Indicate what they do not like about him and why he is bad for their daughter.

Dear Diary **January 14, 1986 (written by Zara's parents)**

Writing Skills: Understanding Points of View

Point of view is the way of looking at a particular subject. For example, in *Dear Diary: A Rocky Road to Love*, we see the same situation from two different points of view: Zara's and Alexon's. It is interesting to look at the same situation from different points of view.

Analyze the following situations from different points of view. In the space provided write how each person sees the action.

1. *Alexon and Zara break up.*
   Alexon:

   Zara

2. *Alexon gets married.*
   Alexon:

   Zara

3. *Alexon gets divorced.*
   Alexon:

   Zara

4. *Zara becomes a Vice-President at Chase Manhattan Bank.*
   Alexon:

   Zara

5. *Zara and Alexon meet again at the health club.*
   Alexon:

   Zara

Writing Assignment 8

Comparison Paragraph

SHE AND I

She is always cold. I am always warm. On summer evenings, when everyone else wears sleeveless dresses, she wears a sweater. In the winter, she turns up the heat very high in the house. Then I walk around in the house with shorts and a tee shirt. She hates the cold, snow, and January winds. She says that I am like a polar bear because I love the cold. When she walks with me in the winter, she wears two heavy sweaters, a big overcoat, two big scarves, and a thick hat. I can barely see her face through all the clothes, but I can hear her complain about the weather.

She loves to go out. She is very extroverted. When she goes to a party with twenty-five strangers, she knows all about them after only twenty minutes. She knows that Kittie O'Brien has three children and that Harriett Johanssen has four ex-husbands. She recognizes that Nestor Gomez has shiny caps on his teeth and that Upton Nicholas is wearing a toupee that looks like a dead animal on his head. On the other hand, I find it difficult to talk to new people. I stay back, waiting for somebody I know to introduce me to people. I am a little shy and unsure of myself. When the party is over, I am very happy. She is sad that her good time is over.

She loves to eat spicy food. When she cooks, she puts a lot of red and black pepper into her dishes. She likes to use a lot of garlic and spices. Even when she makes eggs, she takes down all the little jars from the spice rack and sprinkles them one after another onto the eggs. I prefer natural food without too many spices. When I eat her cooking, I begin to sneeze. When I cook and serve her a nice meal, she tastes it, and then pours salt, pepper, garlic powder, and dried rosemary all over it. She does this with a big smile, so I don't get angry.

© Isabella Altano

She has a dog, a big, furry mess who sleeps on the couch or in our bed. If she goes to bed before I do, the dog is always in my spot. When I try to get into bed, the dog growls and looks me right in the eye. Then he finally moves to her side. I have a cat, a mixed breed that I found at the shelter. The cat is very independent. When I call her, she walks very slowly in the opposite direction.

She loves scary movies. I hate them. I like romantic comedies. She finds them stupid. As a result, we often go to see action / adventure films, which we both enjoy. After the movie, we go to a diner. I drink three cups of coffee and eat a piece of cheesecake. She never drinks coffee after 2:00 in the afternoon. She says that it keeps her awake. She wants to be sophisticated and drink a glass of white wine, but she really prefers milk and chocolate cake, chocolate brownie, chocolate cupcakes, chocolate anything.

We met in the park more than twenty-five years ago. Her dog was biting a jogger, and I stopped to watch her reaction. She apologized again and again, and offered to buy him a new pair of jogging pants. She smiled and the man ran away quickly, afraid of the dog. I stayed to talk to her. We talked for more than an hour. We have talked every day since.

Now we are about to celebrate our thirtieth wedding anniversary. In a world where change happens all the time, we are still together, still happy to be together all the time. I really hope that the future will be more of the same.

Analyzing comparisons

Fill in the chart with information on the differences between "she" and "I."

POINTS OF COMPARISON	OBJECT 1: "SHE"	OBJECT 2: "I"
Difference:		
Difference:		
Difference:		
Difference:		
Difference:		
Difference:		
Difference:		

Answer the following questions with complete sentences.

1. What is the relationship between the narrator and the woman?

2. Do you think that they are very close?

3. What is happening in the last paragraph of the story?

Text-based writing assignment: Write a paragraph in which you compare yourself and another person (a friend or relative). Try to choose a person who is very different from you.

Writing Assignment 9

The Television and Movie Journal

For the next two weeks, monitor the number of hours that you spend watching television or movies. Pay particular attention to the types of programs or films you watch. Do you prefer comedies, action/adventure, romances, performance, sports, or news programs? What percentage of the shows do you watch in English compared to your native language or another language? Do you usually watch films on television, on DVD from rentals, or at the movie theatre itself? Do you own many movies that you re-watch? At the end of the two-week period, answer the questionnaire and write a paragraph describing the experience.

TELEVISION AND MOVIE JOURNAL – WEEK 1

Day 1	Day 2	Day 3
Hours of television watched:	Hours of television watched:	Hours of television watched:
Programs:	Programs:	Programs:
Percentage in English?	Percentage in English?	Percentage in English?
Describe one of the shows:	Describe one of the shows:	Describe one of the shows:
Favorite actor / actress:	Favorite actor / actress:	Favorite actor / actress:
News stories followed:	News stories followed:	News stories followed:
Sports programming: What sport? Who played? Who won? Describe the game.	Sports programming: What sport? Who played? Who won? Describe the game.	Sports programming: What sport? Who played? Who won? Describe the game.
On tv or dvd, or at the movies	On tv or dvd, or at the movies	On tv or dvd, or at the movies

Day 4	Day 5	Day 6	Day 7
Hours of television watched:	Hours of television watched:	Hours of television watched:	Hours of television watched:
Programs:	Programs:	Programs:	Programs:
Percentage in English?	Percentage in English?	Percentage in English?	Percentage in English?
Describe one of the shows:	Describe one of the shows:	Describe one of the shows:	Describe one of the shows:
Favorite actor / actress:	Favorite actor / actress:	Favorite actor / actress:	Favorite actor / actress:
News stories followed:	News stories followed:	News stories followed:	News stories followed:
Sports programming: What sport? Who played? Who won? Describe the game.	Sports programming: What sport? Who played? Who won? Describe the game.	Sports programming: What sport? Who played? Who won? Describe the game.	Sports programming: What sport? Who played? Who won? Describe the game.
Movies watched:	Movies watched:	Movies watched:	Movies watched:
On tv or dvd, or at the movies	On tv or dvd, or at the movies	On tv or dvd, or at the movies	On tv or dvd, or at the movies

TELEVISION AND MOVIE JOURNAL - WEEK 2

Day 1	Day 2	Day 3
Hours of television watched: Programs: Percentage in English? Describe one of the shows: Favorite actor / actress: News stories followed: Sports programming: What sport? Who played? Who won? Describe the game. On tv or dvd, or at the movies	Hours of television watched: Programs: Percentage in English? Describe one of the shows: Favorite actor / actress: News stories followed: Sports programming: What sport? Who played? Who won? Describe the game. On tv or dvd, or at the movies	Hours of television watched: Programs: Percentage in English? Describe one of the shows: Favorite actor / actress: News stories followed: Sports programming: What sport? Who played? Who won? Describe the game. On tv or dvd, or at the movies

Day 4	Day 5	Day 6	Day 7
Hours of television watched: Programs: Percentage in English? Describe one of the shows: Favorite actor / actress: News stories followed: Sports programming: What sport? Who played? Who won? Describe the game. Movies watched: On tv or dvd, or at the movies	Hours of television watched: Programs: Percentage in English? Describe one of the shows: Favorite actor / actress: News stories followed: Sports programming: What sport? Who played? Who won? Describe the game. Movies watched: On tv or dvd, or at the movies	Hours of television watched: Programs: Percentage in English? Describe one of the shows: Favorite actor / actress: News stories followed: Sports programming: What sport? Who played? Who won? Describe the game. Movies watched: On tv or dvd, or at the movies	Hours of television watched: Programs: Percentage in English? Describe one of the shows: Favorite actor / actress: News stories followed: Sports programming: What sport? Who played? Who won? Describe the game. Movies watched: On tv or dvd, or at the movies

TELEVISION AND MOVIE JOURNAL QUESTIONNAIRE

1. How many hours of television did you watch on the average every day? ____
2. Did you watch more or less television on the weekend? _______
3. On what day did you watch the most television? ______
4. What percentage of the programs were in English? ________
5. Favorite type(s) of program(s) [circle up to three]: 1) news 2) sports 3) performance 4) comedy 5) reality 6) action/adventure 7) romance 8) music
6. Least favorite type of program: 1) news 2) sports 3) performance 4) comedy 5) reality 6) action/adventure 7) romance 8) music
7. What was your favorite television show? ________________________________
8. Why? ____
9. Who are your favorite television actors and actresses? ______________________
10. What channel did you watch the most? ____________________________
11. What time of the day did you watch the most television? ______________
12. How many movies did you watch in the two-week period? _____________
13. What percentage of the movies were in English? ________
14. Favorite type(s) of movies [circle up to two]: 1) comedy 2) horror 3) action/adventure 4) romantic 5) musical 6) mystery
15. Least favorite type of movie: 1) comedy 2) horror 3) action/adventure 4) romantic 5) musical 6) mystery
16. What was your favorite movie? _________________________________
17. Who are your favorite television actors and actresses? ______________________
18. Do you think that watching television and movies improves your English? _____
19. Would you consider yourself a serious television and movie watcher? _____
20. Do you have a large-screen television? ___ HD? ____ Cable or satellite television? ____ Surround sound? _____ Big comfortable chairs or couches? _____

Journal-based writing assignment: Write a paragraph in which you describe your television- and movie-watching habits. Analyze which types of programs you watch the most, whether you watch mostly in English or your native language, and whether you think that watching television and movies is a good way to practice and improve English.

When you come to class with your paragraph, be prepared to discuss it in groups of four students and/or with the class as a whole.

UNIT 2: CAUSE AND EFFECT

Cause and effect writing is the result of *critical thinking*. A cause is **why something happened**. An effect is the **outcome of an occurrence**. You realize that all actions have consequences or effects. If you speed on the highway, you might not have enough time to brake if the person in front of you stops suddenly. You may cause an accident. You could even receive a speeding ticket. A change in your eating habits toward a healthier diet might have important effects. You will probably have more energy, lose weight, and generally feel better.

In analyzing causes, you make *inferences* (conclusions based on information). Your classmate arrives in class and her hair and sweatshirt are wet. What caused this? You can *infer* that it is probably raining. She is also yawning continuously. You infer that she did not sleep enough last night. Maybe she worked late. Perhaps she was studying. Maybe she went to a club and came back at three o'clock.

In academic courses and in everyday life, you look for causes of major events. What were the causes of World War II? How did the northern army win the Civil War? How did John F. Kennedy win the presidential election of 1960? You could also examine effects. What is the effect of the dissolution of the Soviet Union into many republics? What is the effect of America's decision to invade Iraq? Will David Beckham's signing with Los Angeles Galaxy have an important effect on U.S. soccer?

Realize that there are usually multiple causes why something happened and several different effects, too. If your favorite team is having a bad year it might be due to injuries to key players, a difficult schedule, and several unlucky bounces, not just bad coaching. The decision to fire the manager may seem like the most logical one, but you can never be sure that it will solve the team's problems.

PARAGRAPH CHART FOR CAUSE AND EFFECT WRITING

Verb tenses used	1. Simple present to discuss causes and effects 2. The simple past tense for specific examples 3. The simple future to project the effects into a future time period
Organization	A listing of causes (effects)—similar to reasons in an opinion paragraph; give three or four causes or effects
Outline	An idea cluster (idea map)
The process from outline to paragraph	1. Brainstorm causes (or effects)—write about eight 2. Narrow the list to the best three or four 3. Use an idea cluster to organize your thoughts 4. Write a strong topic sentence 5. Follow the chart from box to box as you write your paragraph 6. Write a good conclusion
Discourse markers for enumeration	*first, second, third* *the first cause is; the second cause is; the final cause is* *one effect is; another effect might be* Adding information words: *in addition, moreover, furthermore, also*
Discourse markers for cause and effect	*because* and *since* (these two often have the same meaning) *as a result; therefore; consequently* (the same meaning) *Because she is optimistic, she always sees the bright side.* *Since you are always late, we miss the beginning of films.* *Heena studied hard. As a result, she got an A.* *It is raining; therefore, we have to cancel the picnic.* *Mark is a lazy dog; consequently, don't expect him to help.*
Topic sentence	The topic sentence for a cause and effect paragraph introduces the subject and shows whether the writing will look backward or forward. *There are several principal causes of the Vietnam War.* *The effects of global warming are clear in many aspects.* *The changes in the parking lot have affected students most.*
Concluding sentence	The conclusion should present a summary of the issue and perhaps speak of its impact. Begin with *In conclusion* or *For these reasons.* *In conclusion, Al Gore's selection for the Nobel Peace Prize will bring more attention to the problem of global warming.* *For these reasons, the atmosphere in the school is much better because of the improvements in the school cafeteria.*
Spelling note	**Effect**: a count noun (There are many *effects* of the war.) **Affect**: a verb (His negative personality *affects* us all.)

Journal and practice topics

Practice writing idea clusters for the following topics. Then choose one or more topics and write paragraphs.

1. Suppose that you are asked to write an advertising brochure for the English as a Second Language program at your college. Present reasons why your school is an excellent place to study English.
2. There has been a marked increase in violence in schools around the world. Why do you think that students bring guns into school buildings and commit violent acts?
3. Explain why your [town, county, or state] is a wonderful place to live.
4. The divorce rate is rising in most countries. Why is this so?
5. Many young people think they know everything. Do you think that perhaps they are right? Why or why not?
6. Americans do not really stress foreign language instruction as much as many other countries. Present reasons why it might not be essential for Americans to learn a second language.
7. In America, it is possible to raise your social class and earn a great deal of money as long as you are willing to work really hard. What are the effects of this possibility?
8. In order to learn a foreign language better, it is important to distance yourself from people who speak your native language. Why might this be true?
9. Some psychologists say that "pet therapy" is very effective in treating loneliness and depression. Why do you think that getting a dog or a cat might make a person happier?
10. Psychologists also write about "seasonal functional disorder." The idea is that people behave differently according to the season. If they really dislike the cold, for example, they usually get depressed in January and February. On the other hand, in July and August, they are the happiest. Do you personally feel that the weather affects your mood? What are the effects of living in a four-season climate (as in the northern United States) as opposed to a two- or even one-season climate?

Grammar in Context

DISCOURSE MARKERS FOR ENUMERATION AND EXAMPLES

Discourse Markers for Enumeration

Whenever writers use enumeration structure, they are providing a list of reasons, advantages, or negatives. The word *enumeration* comes from the Latin word *numer*, which means "number." To introduce these sentences, we use certain discourse markers. Let's analyze them:

> *There are three advantages to the new language system.* ***First,*** *there are no spelling mistakes.* ***In addition,*** *the words are much shorter.* ***Finally,*** *the language is much more direct.*

The *topic sentence* for an enumeration paragraph often begins with "There are... ." This is followed by a quantity word, usually *several* or *many*, and then the point: advantages, benefits, or reasons. The terms *first, in addition*, and *finally* all begin the sentence and are followed by commas, then a subject and a verb. Generally speaking, enumeration paragraphs introduce **three** reasons, disadvantages, benefits, etc.

Another way of organizing an enumeration paragraph is shown in this example. The topic sentence again uses a quantity word (*many*) and provides the topic [walking to work].

> *Walking to work is beneficial in many ways.* ***One benefit is*** *that you stay in shape.* ***Another positive aspect is*** *that you are seldom late.* ***Lastly,*** *you can enjoy the scenery and smell the fresh air.*

Discourse Markers for Examples

There are three common discourse markers used to provide examples: ***such as, for example,*** and ***for instance.*** They work in different ways. *Such as* is used in the middle of the sentence, without a comma before. It is usually followed by a list. Look at the following sample sentences:

> *There are several international people going to the party* ***such as*** *Joanna, Marius, Inez, and Cosimo.*
> [*such as* is followed by a list of proper nouns]
>
> *Jon found a few ways to make some extra money* ***such as*** *selling his old clothes, working on Sundays at the flea market, and shoveling snow in the winter.* [*such as* is followed by a series of gerunds]
> *I need many things from the supermarket* ***such as*** *milk, butter, and corn.* [list of nouns]

For example and *For instance* always begin a new sentence. They are followed by commas, and then a subject and verb. Analyze these sentences:

> *Working out is good for your soul.* **For example,** *Harold is much happier since he started going to the gym.*
> *There are many beautiful perennials to plant in the garden.* **For instance,** *roses and tulips come back every year and make the garden look wonderful.*

Exercise 1: Transition Practice

Work with a partner to find the relationship in the sentence and choose the correct discourse marker.

1. They had a party _____________ Juan got a promotion.
   a. although b. because c. before d. if

2. There are several things that you can do to increase your earnings. __________, you can work more hours.
   a. Such as b. For example c. As a result d. Next

3. Daniel studied very hard, _______ he got a high grade on the examination.
   a. so b. but c. yet d. while

4. _____________ she was driving to school, Gabriela drank a cup of coffee.
   a. After b. While c. Before d. As soon as

5. ___ you call me, I will come right away.
   a. Until b. While c. Before d. If

6. I don't like your sister. ______________, I don't care for your dog.
   a. However b. But c. So d. In addition

7. Yesi woke up at 6:00. Then she got dressed, had breakfast, washed the dishes, made her bed, and called her mother. _______, she left.
   a. After b. Finally c. Next d. When

8. There are many people to contact _____________ Nancy, Michael, Kelly, and Jo.
   a. such as b. for example c. like as d. who

9. Everyone loves Teresa _______________ she is a genuinely nice person.
   a. because of b. due to c. since d. despite

10. We all got very wet _________________ the sudden rain.
    a. because of b. due to c. since d. despite

Exercise 2: Sentence Completion

Write a conclusion to the following sentences. Punctuate carefully.

1. Because my grandmother doesn't work ____.
2. There are many places I would like to visit such as____________________________________.
3. You can get to my house in many ways for example _____________________________.
4. Since you understand the grammar chapter ______________________________________.
5. You can do several things to relax for instance _______________________________.

The Writing Workout Page

CAUSE AND EFFECT WRITING

In 1978, the average age for first marriage in the United States was 23.8 for men and 21.8 for women. Today, one generation later, the average age is 27.9 for men and 25.3 for women. In fact, the average age for first marriage has increased every year for the last fifty years. The same is true in most countries in the world. Why is this so? What are the causes of people getting married later?	
Another important demographic change is the modification of the family structure. More than 50 percent of marriages end in divorce. Many people marry a second time and have children with their new spouses. As a result, there are stepmothers and stepfathers, stepchildren, stepbrothers and stepsisters, and half-brothers and half-sisters. In addition, there are many more single-parent homes than ever before. What do you feel are the effects of changes in the family structure?	
A common question asked during job interviews is "Why did you choose to become a...? After you finish your English courses, you might continue to study in college. You will choose a major (the course of study on which you will concentrate). What caused you to be interested in your major field?	

You made the important decision to come to the United States to live (unless you were brought here by your parents or a spouse). What are the effects of this occurrence? How has your life changed and how will it change even more as a result of the fact that you have come to America?	____
Some people drink too much. Others smoke. There are those who eat in excess. People gamble even when they do not have enough money. Others take drugs. In general, why do people do things they know are wrong? Why do they ignore simple logic that tells them that doing these things is stupid, unhealthy, and even dangerous?	____

Writing Assignment 1

Self-Analysis

WHY AM I HAPPY OR UNHAPPY?

Some psychologists say that you are happier when you often do activities that you really like. On the other hand, you are probably unhappy if you have to do many things that you do not like. For this exercise, you are going to analyze the activities that you most and least like to do and indicate how often you perform them.

List your four favorite activities (e.g., travel, dancing, gardening, meeting friends).

____________________ ____________________

____________________ ____________________

Use the following sentence constructions to write about your favorite activities:

1. I really like (+ infinitive) — *I really like to have dinner with friends.*
2. I love (+ infinitive) — *I love to cook wonderful meals.*
3. I enjoy (+ gerund) — *I enjoy playing the piano.*
4. I am very happy when (+ S V) — *I am very happy when I watch an exciting movie.*
5. When (S V), I am in a good mood — *When I go dancing, I am in a good mood.*

1. I really love …
2.
3.
4.
5.

Now copy your four favorite activities in the first column of the chart below. In the second column, indicate the last time you did the activity. In the third column, tell how often you do the activity. For example:

ACTIVITY	THE LAST TIME I DID IT	HOW OFTEN I DO IT
Playing soccer with friends	*Last Sunday*	*Every Sunday*

FAVORITE ACTIVITIES CHART

ACTIVITY	THE LAST TIME I DID IT	HOW OFTEN I DO IT

Self-Analysis: Am I Happy? Look at the *Favorite Activities Chart.* When was the last time you did your favorite activities? If it was yesterday, last weekend, or last week, you are probably happy. If you last did your favorite activity four months ago, one year ago, or several years ago, you might be unhappy. For example, suppose you really love to travel. However, recently you have been working a lot and going to school full time. You don't have the time or the money to take a trip. As a result, you are probably sad about this. On the other hand, if you love to go dancing, and you went last Friday night, you are most likely happy.

The same can be said about how frequently you do your other favorite activities. If you really love to go to the movies, but don't have time because you work in the evening, you will not be so happy. On the other hand, if you prefer to work outside in the garden, and you do it every afternoon for one hour, you will most likely be content.

List your least favorite activities (but ones that you have to do). There are things that you must do (duties) that perhaps you do not like. For example, maybe you hate to clean the bathroom, but this is your *chore* at home. You have no choice. You have to do it. List four activities that you really do not enjoy, but that you have to do. (This is not limited to house duties, but may include things you have to do outside the home.)

____________________ ____________________

____________________ ____________________

Use the following sentence constructions to write about your least favorite activities:

1. I really hate (+ infinitive) — *I really hate to drive to the airport.*
2. I don't like (+ infinitive) — *I don't like to work on Saturdays.*
3. I do not enjoy (+ gerund) — *I do not enjoy cooking every night.*
4. I am very unhappy when (+ S V) — *I am very unhappy when I have to wash the dishes.*
5. When (S V), I am in a bad mood — *When I must be nice to rude customers, I am in a bad mood.*

1.
2.
3.
4.
5.

Now copy your four least favorite activities in the first column. In the second column, indicate the last time you did the activity. In the third column, tell how often you do the activity.

LEAST FAVORITE ACTIVITIES CHART

ACTIVITY	THE LAST TIME I DID IT	HOW OFTEN I DO IT

Again, probably the more you have to perform an activity that you hate, the more likely you will be unhappy. You may have to change your attitude, and just accept your responsibility without the negative feelings or try to find a way to switch the unpleasant chore with a family member.

Writing assignment: On a separate sheet of paper, write a paragraph about your favorite and your least favorite activities. Tell how often you do these activities and when the last time was when you did them. Use the structures introduced (e.g., *I really like...*, *I hate...*). Use adverbs of frequency in some of your sentences (*always*, *frequently*, *usually*, *often*, *sometimes*, *rarely*, *seldom*, *almost never*, *never*).

Writing Assignment 2

The Art of Listening and Giving Good Advice

THE STORY OF WU LAO REN

Once upon a time, there was a poor elderly farmer named Wu Lao Ren. He lived in rural China with his wife. They also had a twelve-year-old son. Wu Lao Ren worked very hard, and his back was a little bent. He did not have much money. He grew cabbage, beans, peppers, and scallions on a small farm. He had a few chickens and a very sick pig. Wu Lao Ren's prize possession was his donkey. He took great care of the animal and gave him the same food that the family ate.

One day Wu Lao Ren went to the market to sell his vegetables. On market day, once a week, he brought many cabbages and peppers, so he needed to bring the donkey to help carry them. He woke up very early in the morning and put all the vegetables in a large basket. Wu Lao Ren decided to bring his son to the market, too. The road to the market was very crowded. He and his son walked happily along, and they greeted their friends. The donkey carried the heavy basket on its back.

Wu Lao Ren was very successful this particular day, and he sold all his vegetables. He and his son were ready to take the long trip home. Wu Lao Ren was a little tired. He rode the donkey. When people saw him, they spoke loudly: "Wu Lao Ren is selfish. He is riding the donkey and making the young boy walk all the way home from the market." Wu Lao Ren heard them, so he got off the donkey and he put his son on. When they passed by some other people standing in front of the bread shop, they heard other voices, "How stupid that is! The young and healthy boy is riding the donkey while poor old Wu Lao Ren is walking. The world is really upside down." So the boy got off the donkey, and Wu Lao Ren and his son both walked alongside the donkey. Other people saw them and said, "How stupid that is! Why are they taking a donkey if no one rides it?"

Wu Lao Ren and his son didn't know what to do. So they decided that both of them should ride the donkey. When other people saw the two of them, they said, "How stupid that is! Are they so lazy that neither of them can walk?" Are they trying to kill that poor old donkey? As a result, both Wu Lao Ren and his son got off the donkey. Wu Lao Ren took the front of the donkey and his son took the back of the donkey, and they carried it home.

They arrived tired and unhappy. Wu Lao Ren's wife came out to meet them. She screamed, "What are you doing, you two fools? Are you actually carrying the donkey home?" Wu Lao Ren and his son explained everything that the people said during their trip. Wu Lao Ren's wife, who was an intelligent woman, said, "You must have a mind of your own! Don't always pay attention to what other people say!"

When someone listens to what everyone says and tries to act accordingly, they call him or her "*Wu Lao Ren*" in honor of the clueless farmer who tried to satisfy everyone and ended up carrying his donkey home.

Understanding the passage

Circle the correct answer.

1. The story takes place in:
   a. India. b. China. c. Japan. d. Korea.

2. Wu Lao Ren is a:
   a. farmer. b. merchant. c. store owner. d. grandfather.

3. How many people are in Wu Lao Ren's family?
   a. one b. two c. three d. four

4. Wu Lao Ren's prized possession is his:
   a. pic. b. chicken. c. cabbages. d. donkey.

5. How often is market day?
   a. once a month b. every day c. once a week d. twice a week

6. What did Wu Lao Ren's donkey eat?
   a. hay b. corn c. the same as Wu Lao Ren d. grass

7. One the way to the market, who rides the donkey?
   a. no one b. Wu Lao Ren c. Wu Lao Ren's son d. Wu Lao Ren's wife

8. Who goes to the market?
   a. Wu Lao Ren alone b. Wu Lao Ren, with his wife and son c. Wu Lao Ren and his son

9. Is Wu Lao Ren successful at the market?
   a. no, nobody buys anything b. yes, he sells some fruit c. yes, he sells everything

10. On the way home, who rides the donkey first?
    a. Wu Lao Ren b. Wu Lao Ren's son c. no one d. Wu Lao Ren's wife

11. Who is the second one to ride the donkey?
    a. Wu Lao Ren b. Wu Lao Ren's son c. no one d. Wu Lao Ren's wife

12. What happens when Wu Lao Ren and his son ride the donkey?
    a. everyone is happy
    b. the people say that they are stupid
    c. the donkey is unhappy
    d. Wu Lao Ren's wife is happy

13. How does the donkey get home?
    a. it walks b. it runs c. it carries Wu Lao Ren d. Wu Lao Ren and his son carry it

14. When Wu Lao Ren and his son get home, his wife is:
    a. happy. b. angry. c. nervous. d. sad.

15. Wu Lao Ren's wife thinks that he is:
    a. stupid. b. a good husband. c. kind. d. old.

16. Wu Lao Ren's son is:
    a. twelve. b. fifteen. c. six. d. nine.

17. The moral of the story is:
    a. only listen to your wife.
    b. listen to everybody and try to make them happy.
    c. don't listen to everyone.
    d. don't carry your donkey home.

18. Wu Lao Ren's wife is:
    a. stupid. b. a good wife. c. kind. d. intelligent.

19. The people in the town where Wu Lao Ren lives are:
    a. shy. b. interested in other people's business. c. kind.
    d. not interested in other people's business.

20. What kind of advice does the moral of the story present?
    a. impractical b. practical c. strange d. out-of-date

Text-based writing assignment: One of Wu Lao Ren's main problems is that he tries to listen to everyone and make them all happy. Sometimes, this is impossible. Are you the type of person who listens to other people's advice and acts accordingly? Or are you mostly independent in thought and action? If you listen to others, who are the most important people you try to make happy? Finally, do you feel that the advice given by your elders is always correct because it is based on their lifelong experience? Or do you believe that they might be out-of-touch with modern problems?

Writing Assignment 3

Problem Solving

REDESIGNING THE SCHOOL CAFETERIA

Background: The cafeteria in your college is old. The style is not appealing, and the atmosphere is depressing. There is a cause and effect relationship between the cafeteria space and customer satisfaction. This summer, the school is going to remove everything and completely redesign the space. You are on a committee that represents the students. You have been asked to submit a plan for a new cafeteria.

Group work: Work in groups of four. First, go to your school cafeteria to get some ideas on what works and what doesn't work in design. Then meet as a group to brainstorm ideas about what an excellent cafeteria needs to be attractive to students. A group secretary (elected by the group) should write down the ideas.

Writing assignment: The group will write a paragraph in which you present the ideas discussed. What features should a wonderful cafeteria have? After the group has written the paragraph together, each member should proofread it. Make the changes necessary for a strong paragraph.

Nonverbal communication

(1) Communication takes place is several ways. We can write our friends and families and send them letters, postcards, and email. Telephone calls are another way to keep in touch. The most common way of communicating is by speaking. Most of the time, we are able to understand the meaning of what other people are saying. However, sometimes it is difficult to comprehend them. Maybe they are trying to hide their feelings and don't speak much.

(2) When this happens, we can turn to another way to help us understand: nonverbal communication or body language. There are several important clues that we can find in the way that people use their body when they are speaking. These clues relate to how close people stand to each other during the conversation, what they do with their eyes, how much they touch each other while talking, and the facial expressions they use when they speak.

(3) ***Proxemics*** is the study of where people stand in relation to each other while they are talking. This distance varies from culture to culture. Everyone likes to enjoy a little "personal space." When the other person stands too close during a conversation, this personal space is invaded, and we feel uncomfortable. As a result, we tend to back up. If the other person is accustomed to speaking at a shorter distance, he or she will move closer. This looks like a dance, with one person advancing and the other person retreating.

(4) ***Haptics*** refers to how much people touch each other during conversations. Analyze your own behavior. Do you tend to rest your hand on the shoulder of the people you are talking to? Do you touch their hands, arms, or face? Where do you keep your hands while you are speaking? Again, haptic behavior varies from culture to culture. Generally speaking, the cultures with greater proxemics will have greater haptics. That is, in the cultures in which people stand closer to each other, people will probably touch each other more. In some cultures, touching the other person during a conversation is considered very rude behavior. In other cultures, it is an acceptable, even common sign of friendship and interest.

(5) The study of how the eyes function during conversations is called ***occulesics***. In America, a person shows respect by looking into the eyes of the person speaking. When people (especially children) look away from their parents, teachers, or other authority figures, it is a sign that they are guilty or they are lying. When children are sent to the principal's office in elementary school because they wrote something bad on the blackboard, the students might look down at the floor. "Look me in the eyes," the principal says. "I want to hear the truth!" In class, people are supposed to look at the professor. This action shows respect and interest. When students look all around the room instead concentrating on the professor, it may mean that they are bored. However, in some cultures, as in Asia, it is not polite to look professors or elders in the eyes. Looking down is a sign of respect. Another aspect of occulesics is how long we are supposed to look at another person. Gazing at another person for more than three seconds constitutes "staring," which is considered rude.

(6) Another important aspect of nonverbal communication is facial expression. A smile is the warmest expression. It shows happiness, friendliness, warmth, and liking. People who smile a great deal are considered warm, friendly, and likeable. Sometimes, though, even without thinking, people "make faces." These "faces" shows unhappiness, discontent, and dissatisfaction. "Why did you make a face?" one person asks another.

"What did I do?" the second replies. A message has been sent, even without words. "Making a face" is always negative. Facial expressions can also show if people are interested or bored, angry or content. If you can read faces well, you can tell if the other person understands you or is confused, if the person is following your words or thinking about something else. It is not easy to hide your emotions in your facial expressions. However, if you have a "poker face," you have this ability. This term comes from the card game, poker. If you have a great hand (four aces), you are not supposed to smile or show that you are sure to win. Instead, you try to hide your emotions with a completely blank look.

(7) The ability to understand nonverbal communication is an important one. It can make you a better sender of signals. This is particularly essential for second language speakers. If you comprehend haptics, occulesics, proxemics, and facial expressions, it will make you a better receiver of messages, too. You feel on the same level as the speaker, and this psychological closeness improves communication.

Understanding the text

Choose the correct response to the question.

1. The study of touching behavior during conversations is called:
   a. occulesics.
   b. proxemics.
   c. haptics.
   d. nonverbal communication.

2. The study of eye contact during conversations is called:
   a. occulesics.
   b. proxemics.
   c. haptics.
   d. nonverbal communication.

3. The study of how close we stand to each other during conversations is called:
   a. occulesics.
   b. proxemics.
   c. haptics.
   d. nonverbal communication.

4. According to the article, children often look away from their parents when they:
   a. want to show respect.
   b. are lying.
   c. are telling the truth.
   d. are thinking about something else.

5. According to the article, in Asia, people often look down when they:
   a. want to show respect.
   b. are lying.
   c. are telling the truth.
   d. are thinking about something else.

Analyzing the text

True or false. Indicate whether the sentence is true or false. If it is false, correct it to make it true.

1. ______ Haptic behavior is very consistent around the world.
2. ______ It is considered rude if we look at another person for a long time.
3. ______ The most common method of communication is writing.
4. ______ Latin Americans and Italians usually stand closer to each other when speaking than British and American people.
5. ______ Students should look at their professor only to show respect.

Match the vocabulary word with the definition.

1. ____ comprehend
2. ____ nonverbal communication
3. ____ haptics
4. ____ elders
5. ____ retreat
6. ____ advance
7. ____ proxemics
8. ____ rude
9. ____ occulesics
10. ____ function

a. people older than you are
b. understand
c. to move backwards
d. to move forward
e. very impolite
f. touching behavior during conversations
g. work, operate
h. the distance people stand apart
i. body language
j. eye contact during communication

Focus on Parts of Speech: Review

Tell the parts of speech of the following words from the passage.

1. important (par. 2) ___________
2. relate (par. 2) ___________
3. they (par. 2) ___________
4. personal (par. 3) ___________
5. conversation (par. 3) ___________
6. uncomfortable (par. 3) ___________
7. accustomed (par. 3) ___________
8. during (par. 4) ___________
9. your (par. 4) ___________
10. varies (par. 4) ___________
11. common (par. 4) ___________
12. of (par. 5) ___________
13. especially (par. 5) ___________
14. it (par. 5) ___________
15. respect (par. 5) ___________
16. another (par. 5) ___________
17. rude (par. 5) ___________
18. facial (par. 6) ___________
19. however (par. 6) ___________
20. psychological (p. 7) ___________

Give the connotation—positive (+), negative (-), or neutral (=)—for each word.

1. difficult _____ 2. hide _______ 3. important ______ 4. uncomfortable ___

5. retreating ____ 6. rude _______ 7. likeable _______ 8. warmth _________

9. discontent ____ 10. dissatisfaction ____ 11. blank ________ 12. closeness ______

Writing Skills: Finding the Main Idea of a Paragraph

There are seven paragraphs in *Nonverbal Communication.* Match the paragraph number with the main idea.

1. ____ Paragraph 1
2. ____ Paragraph 2
3. ____ Paragraph 3
4. ____ Paragraph 4
5. ____ Paragraph 5
6. ____ Paragraph 6
7. ____ Paragraph 7

a. introduction to body language
b. how much people touch each other in conversation
c. the function of the eyes in nonverbal communication
d. facial expressions
e. the various types of communication
f. the importance of understanding nonverbal communication
g. how far people stand from each other in conversation

Writing Skills: Analyzing Nonverbal Communication

This week, pay particular attention to the nonverbal communication of a close friend, a classmate, a colleague (co-worker), and a relative. Also rate yourself. Analyze these people in respect to the following aspects. Use the scoring system (1, 2, or 3) indicated by the levels.

proxemics:	1. very close	2. average distance	3. very far away
haptics:	1. always touches	2. sometimes touches	3. never touches
occulesics:	1. close eye contact	2. regular level	3. rarely looks in the eye
facial expression:	1. very expressive	2. normal level	3. poker face (hides expression)

ASPECT	YOU	FRIEND ( )	CLASSMATE ( )	COLLEAGUE OR ANOTHER FRIEND ( )	RELATIVE ( )
Proxemics (1, 2, or 3)					
Haptics (1, 2, or 3)					
Occulesics (1, 2, or 3)					
Facial expression (1, 2, or 3)					
Does this level of nonverbal communication hide or reveal messages?					

Text-based writing assignment: In a clearly written and well-organized paragraph, assess your own nonverbal communication behavior and that of typical people from your culture. Discuss the four elements: proxemics, haptics, occulesics, and facial expression.

Writing Assignment 4

Expressing Yourself with Tattoos

Suppose that you decide to get a tattoo. What is the image that you will choose? Where will you place the tattoo on your body? Will it be bright and colorful? Describe the significance of the image and why you chose it.

Alternate assignment: Pay particular attention to tattoos this week. If you meet people with interesting tattoos, interview them. Ask them why they chose their particular tattoo and what special meaning it has for them.

INVENTING A NEW LANGUAGE

EMAIL, TEXTING, AND INTERNET COMMUNICATION

Dan Altano

(1) The world of technology is ever-changing. Technology allows us to continuously alter and better our lives. There is a constant search to find newer and faster ways to go about everyday activities. As technology changes, people also change along with it. Recently, even the way people communicate with one another has become a lot different. The Internet has made receiving and sharing information faster than ever before. We can now talk to people from all around the world in just a click of a button. Electronic Mail (email) and texting have become popular ways to communicate. Typing instead of speaking to one another has almost become a language all its own. People have learned to abbreviate certain words and phrases in order to speed up an online conversation. This tool helps in many ways such as making quick plans with a friend and running a business.

(2) Sherryl Miller has been working for a design company for many years. In the past, whenever Sherryl needed help with her work or had any questions, she would meet with her boss Ms. Richardson. After the addition of email to her work place, Sherryl can now ask her boss questions without leaving her desk. She types her question in the form of a letter, and then in one click of a button, she sends the letter to her boss Ms. Richardson's *Screen Name.* A screen name is like a mailbox, except instead of sending a letter to a house or an apartment, the email gets sent from one computer to another. Ms. Richardson then opens her email and reads it at her computer. After Ms. Richardson reads Sherryl's question, she answers her right away by returning an email to Sherryl's computer. By using email instead of a face-to-face meeting, Sherryl and Ms. Richardson save a lot of valuable time in the workplace. This is the way companies have begun to go about business all around the world. Instead of taking long flights or spending great amounts of time and money using the phone, clients and customers can use email. Email is the quickest and cheapest way to get in touch with people, no matter where they work or live.

(3) Aside from business, email has become a great way for friends and family members to keep in touch. Steve Mugno lives in Salt Lake City, Utah, but has many family members living in Arizona. By using email, Steve can still stay in closer touch with his family. For example, he can send his best wishes to them on holidays and birthdays and tell them about his new job. Instead of expensive phone bills or waiting a long time for letters to be delivered in the mail, Mugno and his family save time and money. More importantly, Steve stays close with his family and can reach them at any time.

(4) *Texting* is a faster way of communicating than emailing. In order to talk, or "*chat*" with one another, members must be *signed on* and ready to respond immediately. Texting allows people to create a list of friends, relatives, and colleagues to whom they wish to talk. This list is commonly called a *buddy list* or a *contact list.* If a particular person is online and wishes to speak to another person online, they can contact each other by writing a message in a box and sending it. Sending a message opens up a small window where the two friends can type messages to each other that both people can see. The messages are sent within seconds, and people can continue to chat as long as they wish. A big difference between texting and email is that texting uses *real time.* Real time means that messages travel at almost the same speed as a face-to-face or telephone conversation. Texting has become very popular. In college dormitories, students are able to communicate from room to room without having to leave their desks. College students can also have online conversations with their high school friends who are attending different universities. It also works between

working parents and children. For instance, when Jerome Bigsby wants to remind his daughter Jane that she has a music lesson, he simply instant messages her from his office to her computer at home. "It is the easiest way to talk with my family when I can't be with them," says Jerome.

(5) There are many positive aspects to that fast world of communication. First, people have begun to abbreviate the English language in order to speed up conversations. For example, the four-word expression I do not know is often times shortened and written like the word would sound if you were speaking it. I do not know then becomes "I dunno." Some people have even gone as far as shortening the expression further. Instead of I don't know, the expression is abbreviated by taking the first letter of each word, leaving the three-letter symbol IDK. This tool is used in many common phrases in the English language (see abbreviations chart). Abbreviating words and phrases saves time. Second, people are able to communicate faster and get their point across more quickly than ever. The Internet has become so popular, that this new way of speaking has almost become a language of its own. The language has also extended to text messages on cellphones. Because people are spending more and more time on the Internet and cellphones than ever before, it will be interesting to see how the English language will change in the coming years. Finally, there are no spelling mistakes in texting. The words are spelled for the most part as they are pronounced. Also, because the language is less formal, writers do not have to worry about spelling.

(6) There are also some negative sides to the way people are communicating online. First of all, when students learn how to read and write the English language, they learn about proper grammar, punctuation, spelling, and syntax rules. What is happening with email and texting is that when people begin to abbreviate and change the language to save time, they are practicing a language in a highly informal way. For instance, sentences written in email or texting often do not have periods, commas, or apostrophes. Rules of capitalizing letters at the beginning of sentences are commonly ignored, and so is proper spelling. The risk in letting this new way of reading and writing become too popular is that people will have difficulty seeing the difference between Instant Message and Email English and Standard English.

(7) People are starting to write much more than they did ten years ago. Texting and email have made writing immediate, dramatic, and also fun. Online writers are enjoying themselves with language. They invent new terms and phrases every day. They express their emotions—love, anger, disappointment—in real-time messages. And the results baffle some English teachers and most parents. 911 is the code term in texting for "My parent is coming into the room" (911 is the emergency telephone number). It is this urgency, this desire to create a language all its own, that makes the language of texting and Email so fascinating.

TEXTING SLANG	STANDARD WRITTEN ENGLISH
wat^ / waz^ u	What's up?
nmjc, u	Nothing much just chilling, you? [chilling means *relaxing*]
b/c	Because
mi	My
2 / tu	To
sed	Said
riting	Writing
l8ter	Later
bout	About
tha	The
fone	Phone
h/o	hold on
brb	be right back
ttyl	talk to you later
c ya	see you
lov ya / l...u	love you
waz	Was
bbl	be back later
nd	And
doin	Doing
notin	Nothing
kelw / kool	Cool
yup / ya / yea	Yes
rite	Right
be4	Before
im	I'm
1 sec.	one second
havin	Having
sumthin	Something
sumtim	Sometime
lil	Little
gurl	Girl
alrite	Alright
nvm	Nevermind
y	Why
u	You

fyi	for your information
lol	laugh out loud
lmao	laughing my ass off
rotfl	rolling on the floor laughing
some1	Someone
anybody	Anybody
cri	Cry
cryin	Crying
shut^	shut up
so wat	so what
leest	Least
Hert	Hurt
4get	Forget
idk	I don't know
bi	bye / buy / by
g2g	got to go
getting	Getting
leavin	Leaving
omg	Oh my god / Oh my gosh

Chart prepared by Erica Cirilli

Vocabulary Skills: Identifying Discourse Markers
Find the following discourse markers in the passage.

1. Paragraph 1: a discourse marker for example: ______________________
2. Paragraph 2: a discourse marker for example: ______________________
3. Paragraph 3: a discourse marker for example: ______________________
4. Paragraph 5: a topic sentence for enumeration: ______________________
   ____
5. Paragraph 5: the first discourse marker for enumeration: ______________________
6. Paragraph 5: a discourse marker for example: ______________________
7. Paragraph 5: the second discourse marker for enumeration: ______________________
8. Paragraph 5: the third discourse marker for enumeration: ______________________
9. Paragraph 6: another topic sentence for enumeration: ______________________
   ____
10. Paragraph 6: the first discourse marker for enumeration: ______________________

Vocabulary Matching

Match the words with their correct definition.

1. ____ texting
2. ____ signed on
3. ____ real time
4. ____ chat
5. ____ buddy list
6. ____ contact list
7. ____ IDK
8. ____ abbreviate
9. ____ ignore
10. ____ baffle

a. to make shorter
b. not pay attention to
c. to talk informally
d. a list of friends for online chats
e. to completely confuse
f. registered online
g. sending messages in real time
h. a list of business associates
i. in actual time
j. I don't know

Writing Skills: Finding the Main Idea of a Paragraph

There are seven paragraphs in the passage. Match the paragraph number with the main idea.

1. ____ Paragraph 1
2. ____ Paragraph 2
3. ____ Paragraph 3
4. ____ Paragraph 4
5. ____ Paragraph 5
6. ____ Paragraph 6
7. ____ Paragraph 7

a. texting
b. email and the family
c. email in business
d. new forms of communication
e. Texting English: a fascinating language
f. positive aspects
g. negative aspects

Text-based Writing Assignment: Putting into Practice What You've Read

A. Work together with a partner for this activity. Either go into the computer lab or the library at school or go online at home. Add your partner to your buddy list. Have a chat using texting. You can do this with several members of the class.

B. Get the email address of several of your classmates. Exchange email messages. Email writing is slightly more formal than texting because it is not done in real time. Also, email messages may be reread and saved, so you should probably pay more attention to spelling and correct grammar. Write messages and responses to classmates.

A challenging, difficult, and out-of-the ordinary assignment

C. Although it is against common practice, try to use perfect grammar and spelling in your writing in emails, chats, instant messages, and text messages for one week. Record the reactions of your friends, classmates, and relatives to your "excellent language" use. Try not to use shortcuts or abbreviations; do not use slang words. Make a strong attempt to use only standard written English in your communications.

Writing Assignment 5

Cause and Effect Writing

Some people are afraid of heights. Others fear snakes. Some are terrified of closed spaces like elevators or closets. Tell what you are afraid of? Why do you have this fear? Did something happen to you when you were young that makes you so afraid now? If you do not have any fears, ask other people and write about their *phobias.*

Writing Assignment 6

The Best and Worst Years of Your Life

Without a doubt, 2007 was the best year of Al Gore's life. In February, the former vice-president to Bill Clinton won the Oscar, the Academy Award for best documentary film for *An Inconvenient Truth*. In October, Gore won an even greater honor: he was awarded the Nobel Peace Prize for his dedication to solving the problem of global warming.

On the other hand, the year 2000 was certainly one of the worst for Vice-President Gore. It was in that year that he lost a very close election for president to George W. Bush. He has probably spent a great deal of time analyzing the causes of his defeat in the election. Some Americans have examined the effects of his loss.

Your best and worst years are probably not as dramatic as Vice-President Gore's. However, they are just as significant. Outline the important occurrences in these years. Also, indicate how the best and worst years have had an effect on your life.

Outline:

Best Year: __________
Significant personal achievements:

Effects:

Worst Year: __________
Significant happenings:

Effects:

Writing Assignment 7

The Computer and Cellphone Use Journal

For the next two weeks, monitor the number of hours that you spend using your computer and your cellphone. For the computer, pay particular attention to the websites that you visit, how many times per day you check your email, how many emails you send and receive per day, and how many chats you have. For the cellphone, check how many calls you make and receive each day, how long the calls last on the average, who you talk to, and why. At the end of the two-week period, answer the questionnaire and write a paragraph describing the experience.

COMPUTER AND CELLPHONE USE JOURNAL – WEEK 1

Day 1	Day 2	Day 3
Hours spent on the computer: Websites visited: Percentage in English? Did you read the news on the internet? If yes, what were the lead stories? Number of email messages sent: Number of email messages received: Number of chats (IM): **Cellphone Use:** Number of calls made: Number of calls received: Total time spent on the phone: How many different people did you speak with today? Number of text messages:	Hours spent on the computer: Websites visited: Percentage in English? Did you read the news on the internet? If yes, what were the lead stories? Number of email messages sent: Number of email messages received: Number of chats (IM): **Cellphone Use:** Number of calls made: Number of calls received: Total time spent on the phone: How many different people did you speak with today? Number of text messages:	Hours spent on the computer: Websites visited: Percentage in English? Did you read the news on the internet? If yes, what were the lead stories? Number of email messages sent: Number of email messages received: Number of chats (IM): **Cellphone Use:** Number of calls made: Number of calls received: Total time spent on the phone: How many different people did you speak with today? Number of text messages:

Day 4	Day 5	Day 6	Day 7
Hours spent on the computer: Websites visited: Percentage in English? Did you read the news on the internet? If yes, what were the lead stories? Number of email messages sent: Number of email messages received: Number of chats (IM): **Cellphone Use:** Number of calls made: Number of calls received: Total time spent on the phone: How many different people did you speak with today? Number of text messages:	Hours spent on the computer: Websites visited: Percentage in English? Did you read the news on the internet? If yes, what were the lead stories? Number of email messages sent: Number of email messages received: Number of chats (IM): **Cellphone Use:** Number of calls made: Number of calls received: Total time spent on the phone: How many different people did you speak with today? Number of text messages:	Hours spent on the computer: Websites visited: Percentage in English? Did you read the news on the internet? If yes, what were the lead stories? Number of email messages sent: Number of email messages received: Number of chats (IM): **Cellphone Use:** Number of calls made: Number of calls received: Total time spent on the phone: How many different people did you speak with today? Number of text messages:	Hours spent on the computer: Websites visited: Percentage in English? Did you read the news on the internet? If yes, what were the lead stories? Number of email messages sent: Number of email messages received: Number of chats (IM): **Cellphone Use:** Number of calls made: Number of calls received: Total time spent on the phone: How many different people did you speak with today? Number of text messages:

COMPUTER AND CELLPHONE USE JOURNAL – WEEK 2

Day 1
Hours spent on the computer:

Websites visited:

Percentage in English?

Did you read the news on the internet?
If yes, what were the lead stories?

Number of email messages sent:
Number of email messages received:

Number of chats (IM):

Cellphone Use:
Number of calls made:
Number of calls received:
Total time spent on the phone:
How many different people did you speak with today?
Number of text messages:

Day 2
Hours spent on the computer:

Websites visited:

Percentage in English?

Did you read the news on the internet?
If yes, what were the lead stories?

Number of email messages sent:
Number of email messages received:

Number of chats (IM):

Cellphone Use:
Number of calls made:
Number of calls received:
Total time spent on the phone:
How many different people did you speak with today?
Number of text messages:

Day 3
Hours spent on the computer:

Websites visited:

Percentage in English?

Did you read the news on the internet?
If yes, what were the lead stories?

Number of email messages sent:
Number of email messages received:

Number of chats (IM):

Cellphone Use:
Number of calls made:
Number of calls received:
Total time spent on the phone:
How many different people did you speak with today?
Number of text messages:

Day 4
Hours spent on the computer:

Websites visited:

Percentage in English?

Did you read the news on the internet?
If yes, what were the lead stories?

Number of email messages sent:
Number of email messages received:

Number of chats (IM):

Cellphone Use:
Number of calls made:
Number of calls received:
Total time spent on the phone:
How many different people did you speak with today?
Number of text messages:

Day 5
Hours spent on the computer:

Websites visited:

Percentage in English?

Did you read the news on the internet?
If yes, what were the lead stories?

Number of email messages sent:
Number of email messages received:

Number of chats (IM):

Cellphone Use:
Number of calls made:
Number of calls received:
Total time spent on the phone:
How many different people did you speak with today?
Number of text messages:

Day 6
Hours spent on the computer:

Websites visited:

Percentage in English?

Did you read the news on the internet?
If yes, what were the lead stories?

Number of email messages sent:
Number of email messages received:

Number of chats (IM):

Cellphone Use:
Number of calls made:
Number of calls received:
Total time spent on the phone:
How many different people did you speak with today?
Number of text messages:

Day 7
Hours spent on the computer:

Websites visited:

Percentage in English?

Did you read the news on the internet?
If yes, what were the lead stories?

Number of email messages sent:
Number of email messages received:

Number of chats (IM):

Cellphone Use:
Number of calls made:
Number of calls received:
Total time spent on the phone:
How many different people did you speak with today?
Number of text messages:

Computer and cellphone use journal questionnaire

Computer Use

1. How many hours did you spend on the computer on the average every day? ______
2. Did you use the computer more or less on the weekend? _______
3. On what day did you use the computer the most? ______
4. What percentage of your computer use was in English? ________
5. Favorite websites: ______________________, ______________________, ______________________, ______________________.
6. How many emails did you send on an average day? ______
7. How many emails did you receive on an average day? ______
8. How many instant messages did you send? ________
9. Did you use the Internet to practice your English (specific language learning websites)? _________
   List websites: ___________________, ______________________
10. Did you read the news on the computer? _____
11. Did you play games on the computer? _____
12. Did you use the computer for anything else? _____
    Describe: ____

Cellphone Use

1. How many calls did you make on an average day? ______
2. How many calls did you receive on an average day? ______
3. What percentage of the time did you speak in English? ________
4. How many text messages did you send on an average day? ______
5. How many minutes / hours per day did you spend on the cellphone? ____

Journal-based writing assignment: Write a paragraph in which you describe your computer and cellphone habits. Analyze which websites you regularly visit, whether you watch mostly in English or your native language, and how you consider the computer primarily: an entertainment tool, a method of communicating with your friends and relatives, a learning instrument, or a way to get news, sports, and weather information. In terms of cellphone use, how important is the cellphone to your everyday life? Could you live without a cellphone? Who do you speak with regularly? Write one paragraph about your computer use and one paragraph about your cellphone use.

When you come to class with your paragraphs, be prepared to discuss them in groups of four students and/ or with the class as a whole.

Lightning Source UK Ltd.
Milton Keynes UK
UKHW051021240123
415873UK00004B/104